YORKSHIRE WEST RIDING

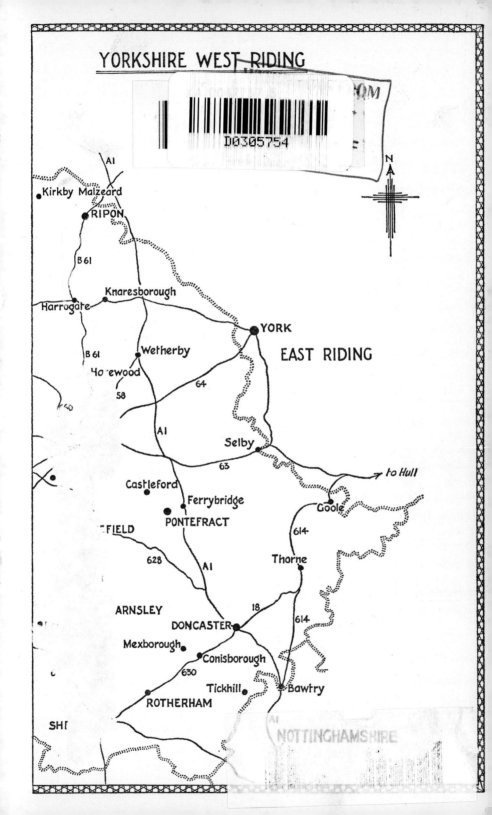

West Riding of Yorkshire

by

ARTHUR RAISTRICK

HODDER AND STOUGHTON

Copyright © 1970 by Arthur Raistrick

First printed 1970

SBN 340 02372 4

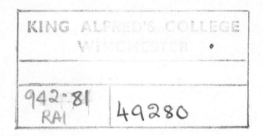
Printed in Great Britain for Hodder and Stoughton Limited, St. Paul's House, Warwick Lane, London, E.C.4 by The Camelot Press Limited, London and Southampton

Contents

List of plates

West Riding of Yorkshire

List of diagrams

Editor's Introduction

SOME SIXTEEN YEARS ago I wrote: "Despite the multitude of books about English landscape and scenery, and the flood of topographical books in general, there is not one book which deals with the historical evolution of the landscape as we know it. At the most we may be told that the English landscape is the man-made creation of the seventeenth and eighteenth centuries, which is not even a quarter-truth, for it refers only to country houses and their parks and to the parliamentary enclosures that gave us a good deal of our modern pattern of fields, hedges, and by-roads. It ignores the fact that more than a half of England never underwent this kind of enclosure, but evolved in an entirely different way, and that in some regions the landscape had been virtually completed by the eve of the Black Death. No book exists to describe the manner in which the various landscapes of this country came to assume the shape and appearance they now have, why the hedgebanks and lanes of Devon should be so totally different from those of the Midlands, why there are so many ruined churches in Norfolk or so many lost villages in Lincolnshire, or what history lies behind the winding ditches of the Somerset marshlands, the remote granite farmsteads of Cornwall, and the lonely pastures of upland Northamptonshire.

"There are indeed some good books on the geology that lies behind the English landscape, and these represent perhaps the best kind of writing on the subject we have yet had, for they deal with facts and are not given to the sentimental and formless slush which afflicts so many books concerned only with superficial appearances. But the geologist, good though he may be, is concerned with only one

aspect of the subject, and beyond a certain point he is obliged to leave the historian and geographer to continue and complete it. He explains to us the bones of the landscape, the fundamental structure that gives form and colour to the scene and produces a certain kind of topography and natural vegetation. But the flesh that covers the bones, and the details of the features, are the concern of the historical geographer, whose task it is to show how man has clothed the geological skeleton during the comparatively recent past —mostly within the last fifteen centuries, though in some regions much longer than this."

In 1955 I published *The Making of the English Landscape*. There I claimed that it was a pioneer study, and if only for that reason it could not supply the answer to every question. Four books, in a series published between 1954 and 1957, filled in more detail for the counties of Cornwall, Lancashire, Gloucestershire, and Leicestershire.

Much has been achieved since I wrote the words I have quoted. Landscape-history is now taught in some universities, and has been studied for many parts of England and Wales in university theses. Numerous articles have been written and a few books published, such as Alan Harris's *The Rural Landscape of the East Riding 1700–1850* (1961) and more recently Dorothy Sylvester's *The Rural Landscape of the Welsh Borderland* (1969).

Special mention should perhaps be made of a number of landscape-studies in the series of Occasional Papers published by the Department of English Local History at the University of Leicester. Above all in this series one might draw attention to *Laughton: a study in the Evolution of the Wealden Landscape* (1965) as a good example of a microscopic scrutiny of a single parish, and Margaret Spufford's *A Cambridgeshire Community (Chippenham)* published in the same year. Another masterly study of a single parish which should be cited particularly is Harry Thorpe's monograph entitled *The Lord and the Landscape*, dealing with the Warwickshire parish of Wormleighton, which also appeared in 1965.[1] Geographers were quicker off the mark than historians in this new field, for it lies on the frontiers of both disciplines. And now botany has been recruited into the field, with the recent development of theories about the dating of hedges from an analysis of their vegetation.

But a vast amount still remains to be discovered about the man-made landscape. Some questions are answered, but new questions continually arise which can only be answered by a microscopic examination of small areas even within a county. My own perspective has enlarged greatly since I published my first book on the subject. I now believe that some features in our landscape today owe their origin to a much more distant past than I had formerly thought possible. I think it highly likely that in some favoured parts of England farming has gone on in an unbroken continuity since the Iron Age, perhaps even since the Bronze Age; and that many of our villages were first settled at the same time. In other words, that underneath our old villages, and underneath the older parts of these villages, there may well be evidence of habitation going back for some two or three thousand years. Conquests only meant in most places a change of landlord for better or for worse, but the farming life went on unbroken, for even conquerors would have starved without its continuous activity. We have so far failed to find this continuity of habitation because sites have been built upon over and over again and have never been wholly cleared and examined by trained archaeologists.

At the other end of the time-scale the field of industrial archaeology has come into being in the last few years, though I touched upon it years ago under the heading of Industrial Landscapes. Still, a vast amount more could now be said about this kind of landscape.

[1] *Transactions of the Birmingham Archaeological Society*, Vol. 80, 1965.

Purists might say that the county is not the proper unit for the study of landscape-history. They would say perhaps that we ought to choose individual and unified regions for such an exercise; but since all counties, however small, contain a wonderful diversity of landscape, each with its own special history, we get, I am sure, a far more appealing book than if we adopted the geographical region as our basis.

The authors of these books are concerned with the ways in which men have cleared the natural woodlands, reclaimed marshland, fen, and moor, created fields out of a wilderness, made lanes, roads, and footpaths, laid out towns, built villages, hamlets, farmhouses and cottages, created country houses and their parks, dug mines and made canals and railways, in short with everything that has altered the natural landscape. One cannot understand the English landscape and enjoy it to the full, apprehend all its wonderful variety from region to region (often within the space of a few miles), without going back to the history that lies behind it. A commonplace ditch may be the thousand-year-old boundary of a royal manor; a certain hedge-bank may be even more ancient, the boundary of a Celtic estate; a certain deep and winding lane may be the work of twelfth-century peasants, some of whose names may be made known to us if we search diligently enough. To discover these things, we have to go to the documents that are the historians' raw material, and find out what happened to produce these results and when, and precisely how they came about.

But it is not only the documents that are the historian's guide. One cannot write books like these by reading someone else's books, or even by studying records in a muniment room. The English landscape itself, to those who know how to read it aright, is the richest historical record we possess. There are discoveries to be made in it for which no written documents exist, or have ever existed. To write the history of the English landscape requires a combination of documentary research and of fieldwork, of laborious scrambling on foot wherever the trail may lead. The result is a new kind of history which it is hoped will appeal to all those who like to travel intelligently, to get away from the guide-book show-pieces now and then, and to know the reasons behind what they are looking at. There is no part of England, however unpromising it may appear at first sight, that is not full of questions for those who have a sense of the past. So much of England is still unknown and unexplored. Fuller enjoined us nearly three centuries ago

"Know most of the rooms of thy native country
before thou goest over the threshold thereof.
Especially seeing England presents thee with
so many observables."

These books on The Making of the English Landscape are concerned with the observables of England, and the secret history that lies behind them.

Exeter, 1970   W. G. HOSKINS

1. Introduction

Physical character

THE WEST RIDING of Yorkshire, though only one of the three Ridings into which the whole of Yorkshire is divided, is a complete administrative unit controlled by a County Council and can be referred to as a county. The area of nearly 2800 square miles stretches ninety miles north-west to south-east from Sedbergh and the Howgill Fells to Doncaster near the Southern border. The Howgill Fells reach over 2000 feet above sea level while much of the land near Doncaster is only a few feet above the sea. More than half of the total area of the West Riding lies on the Pennines, separated from the low-lying plain of the vales of York and Trent which form the eastern part of the county by a fairly narrow belt of foothills. The great topographical differences of mountains above 2000 feet O.D., broad expanses of moorlands above 1000 feet, and Pennine slopes coming down to wide areas of valley lands below 200 feet have ensured a diversity of scenery, climate, and soil which is enjoyed by few other counties. This variety makes it almost impossible to generalise about the area and compels one to seek natural or cultural and industrial zones as the bases for comparisons and discussion. The topography conforms approximately to the broad lines of the geology and the geology contributes much to the character of the soils and provides natural resources of minerals and building materials and so has had a considerable influence on the history of the man-made landscape.

First let us define the area by its natural regions and then look at the settlement and occupational zones which are related to them. The broad upfold of the Pennines has its axis north to south so that the natural regions also tend to keep close to a north to south arrangement. The oldest rocks are those which are revealed in the narrow valleys of the Ingleton Glens, and which are pre-Cambrian in age. The scenery of the glens with their abundant waterfalls is a great tourist attraction, but the total outcrop of these rocks is very small and of no significance in the overall picture. The next oldest rocks are those of the Howgill Fells and the Rawthey and Lune valleys, slaty rocks related to those of the Lake District. These abut against the west side of the Pennines along the Dent Fault which extends from Brough under Stainmore to a little east of Kirkby Lonsdale. The Howgill Fells are a group of smooth-flanked and grass-covered hills rising to a central point in the Calf, 2220 feet, free from walls and fences and forming a vast common sheep pasture. Across the Lune valley on the west, similar fells connect them with the Lake District, but on the east, across the Rawthey valley, the broad fells and dales of the true Pennines offer a strong contrast.

A through valley extends across the Pennines from Skipton in Airedale into Ribblesdale near Settle, then by the valley of the river Wenning into Lunesdale. This through valley route is the Aire Gap, broad and occupied by a maze of drumlins, and forming the Craven Lowlands. North of this 'gap', the north side of which is emphasised by the Craven Faults, the Pennine mass is a high plateau of rocks of Lower Carboniferous age, mainly limestone and shale. The general level of this plateau is between 1000 and 2000 feet with many peaks over 2000 feet such as Ingleborough, 2373 feet, Whernside 2419 feet, and Penygent 2273 feet, and wide areas of moorland tops near the 2000 feet level. This plateau is penetrated by the long and narrow Yorkshire Dales of which Nidderdale, Wharfedale, Airedale, Ribbles-

dale, Dentdale, and Garsdale are in the West Riding
(Plate 1).

South of the river Wenning and west of Ribblesdale is
the great dome of Bowland drained in part by the river
Hodder and its tributaries, itself tributary to the Ribble.
Geologically this mass of fells is allied to the Pennines south
of the Aire Gap. The southern Pennines are generally only
about 1000 to 1200 feet above sea level and are mainly made
of Millstone Grit strata, coarse sandstones, and shales,
which support extensive moors of heather, cotton grass,
and peat. The valleys which penetrate them are shorter
and steeper sided than those to the north and are charac-
terised by the sandstone 'edges' of the Millstone Grit
which contrast strongly with the white limestone scars of
Craven.

Down the east flank of the Pennines, from Ripon to
Doncaster there is a ridge of Magnesian Limestone of
Permian age, four or five miles wide with a well-marked
scar to the west and dipping gently eastward beneath the
Trias marls and sandstones of the vales of York and Trent.
The west-facing escarpment is steep and sometimes rises as
much as 200 feet above the ground to the west. In all its
length this prominent limestone belt forms a landscape of
richer farm land and well wooded parks. A large area of
country between this ridge and the Millstone Grit moors
and to the South of Airedale, is occupied by the Yorkshire
coalfield. This is about twenty-five miles wide along its
northern margin in Airedale, narrowing to about half that
width near Sheffield.

To the east of the limestone ridge the land is very low,
often not more than a few feet above sea level. The Trias
rocks are covered almost everywhere by glacial sands and
gravels and by alluvium and in the lower valleys of the Don
and Trent there are the remains of the widespread flooded
marshes of Hatfield and Thorne and the Humberhead

Fig. 1. Geological divisions of the West Riding.

marshes, much of them only recently drained[1] (Fig. 1).

The climate of the West Riding accords fairly closely with the topography. The rainfall on the higher north-western fells amounts to sixty to seventy inches a year reducing to about twenty-five inches on the south Pennines; in the low ground of the vales of York and Trent the rainfall is less than twenty-five inches. The incidence of wind, cloud, and snow cover effectually prevents arable cultivation on much of the Pennines, the arable being now restricted to the eastern parts of the Riding with some parts of the coalfield and eastern foothills. The soils are varied—on the limestone fells north of the Aire Gap the fine turf up to the base of the Millstone Grits has for many centuries provided a rich sheep-grazing area. The lower Millstone Grit plateau of the south-west carries heather and coarse grasses and so its pasture is much the poorer but provides grazing both for sheep and cattle.

The coalfield provides good woodland soils easily improved where low enough, to support arable farming or mixed dairy farming. It is the strip of Magnesian Limestone, however, with its well drained soil which, along with a better climate and low altitude has given rise throughout its length to a belt of rich farm and park lands. The eastern lowlands have a rich soil derived from the glacial sands, gravels, and clays, combined with marls and sands of the Trias and with a great spread of river alluvium on the extensive river flood plains. Where drainage has recovered land in this area it has produced corn land of very high quality, with a deep rich soil. There are still, however, some areas of unreclaimed land which form Thorne Moss, the Humberhead marshes and some other areas of fen or peat.

The nature of the topography and the soils with their influence upon the vegetation and their relation to the river

[1] P. F. Kendall and H. E. Wroot, *Geology of Yorkshire*, 1924; D. Wray, 'The Pennines and adjacent areas', *British Regional Geology*, 1936.

pattern has dominated the early settlement until mediaeval times, and the occurrence of natural resources of coal, stone, iron, and soft water, among others, have affected the post-mediaeval development of population centres and industry. The present-day pattern of these in the West Riding thus shows a close correspondence with that of the topography and geology. The Riding can be divided into areas which have surprisingly sharp boundaries, so that one steps out of one area into another with a minimum of transition and intermingling. In fact one of the joys of the West Riding is that even in the heaviest industrial areas a short journey enables one to move quickly out of an ugly townscape into a beautiful countryside.

In studying its landscape-history we can take the Riding as being composed of four divisions based upon occupation —agriculture, textiles, coal-mining and steel.[2] Nearly ninety per cent of the total population lives in the areas outside the zone of agriculture although that zone covers more than half of the Riding. The agricultural areas show the greatest variation in the character of occupation, ranging from highland hill farming based upon sheep breeding and grazing, through mixed dairy farming and stock, to large-scale intensive arable farms. The hill farming zone occupies the north-west and much of the Craven dales, with the summit region of the Pennines down the west of the whole Riding (Plate 2). The mixed dairy farming occupies the mid and lower dales and the lower slopes of the Pennines in a broad belt roughly north to south down the Millstone Grit and the Coal Measures (Plate 3). The arable belt is mainly below 250 feet and on the east of the Pennines. It extends over the Magnesian Limestone outcrop and the vales of York and Trent and creeps westward on to the eastern part of the coalfield. There is much drained and

[2] These are the subdivisions adopted by the West Riding County Council in 'A growth policy for the North', *County Development Plan*. Second Review, 1966.

reclaimed land in this zone. It is essentially the area of village and small market towns (Fig. 2).

The textile zone is a vast conurbation. Leeds—Bradford—Halifax—Huddersfield—Wakefield, eighteen miles by fifteen miles, and many smaller towns set in between the larger. There is a small fringe to this area which extends up Airedale to Keighley and up the Calder valley to Hebden Bridge as well as in the Colne valley around Huddersfield. It is very compact and lies almost entirely on the north part of the coalfield. On the south end of the coalfield the third zone, that of steel and iron making, is a smaller area, very compact and extending down the Don valley from Sheffield through Rotherham to Mexborough.

Fig. 2. Occupational zones of the West Riding.

The coalfield of course includes both textile and steel areas although not many collieries are now at work in the western part of it. Most of the collieries were working in the early nineteenth century and pits were then found within both the textile and the steel areas. The trend of the twentieth century has been to extend the coalfield working into the 'concealed area' to the east where the coal measures dip beneath and are covered by newer rocks, and where pits are much deeper, more widely spaced, and are sunk within the arable zone. The intermediate part of the coalfield, the Middle Coal Measures, on the immediate west of the Magnesian Limestone, was worked in the later part of the nineteenth century and still has many working collieries, though these are the ones at present suffering gradual closure.

When man made his first explorations of the area the landscape was one of nearly continuous forest and swamp, except perhaps for only the highest parts of the Pennines. The valleys were occupied by the remnants of glacial lakes, the vales of York and Trent were uncrossable marsh and fen except at the York and Escrick glacial moraines.[3] Only the fairly thin and open scrub along the gritstone edges and the limestone terraces of Craven presented open land along which the Mesolithic hunters could travel. Until the late Neolithic period about the opening of the second millennium B.C. the humans were absorbed into the natural landscape, moving under cover of the forests and making no mark upon it beyond the first faint trackways high on the valley sides. Towards this date of 2000 B.C. the first noticeable man-made landscape was emerging as tiny clearings in the woodland, made by tree felling and perhaps by burning, and continued by grazing animals, sheep and goats. These clearings were no more than tiny islands surrounded by a mass of forest.

[3] A. Raistrick, 'The Bronze Age in West Yorkshire', *Yorkshire Archaeological Journal*, XXIX, 1929, map, Fig. 11, p. 365.

To the north-east of Ripon, on the border of the Riding but just in the North Riding, on the long spur of glacial sands and gravel on the east of the river Ure, there is a group of what are called 'henge' monuments, six of them within seven miles. They are circular platforms of earthwork, with a big ditch and bank outside it, and up to 1500 feet or more in diameter, the ditch being crossed in one or more places by a causeway. Excavation has proved that the circular platform carried a circle or more than one circle of posts making a fairly open but very imposing structure. These places may have been used for the performance of fertility rites and would be centres at which a large and widespread community gathered from time to time. These 'henges' stretching in a line south from Hutton Moor had a wide network of tracks connecting them with scattered settlements the remains of many of which are recognisable, but none of which in themselves are big enough to make any impact on the landscape. By their size and nature and the ceremonies connected with them the 'henges' set in a large cleared area on a high part of the ground must have been easily visible and a prominent feature over many miles of country.

It was not until nearly twenty centuries later that an Iron Age population occupied most of the Pennines and carried the clearance of the woodland very much further, particularly on the limestone and grit terraces where areas of primitive fields were being cultivated. Sheep and cattle were domesticated and bred, and there is even some evidence of a trade in wool. A typical area is that on Lea Green, near Grassington in Wharfedale.[4] There a system of oblong fields, with huts and fragments of a road system among them and a slightly later village of huts and cattle pounds, cover over 300 acres of limestone pasture. The material finds from this area include pottery ranging in date from the second to the early fifth centuries: spindle whorls, weaving combs, and

[4] A. Raistrick, 'Iron Age Settlements in West Yorkshire', *Yorkshire Archaeological Journal*, XXXIV, 1939, pp. 115–50.

loom weights were connected with cloth-making, and knives and other articles of iron were everyday tools. Such sites as this one, but usually less in acreage, are very common over all the limestone area and are present on some of the grit country.

By the first century of the Christian era the people of these 'Celtic' fields were organised in a tribal confederation, the Brigantes, with a ruling caste over them. From them we have inherited constructions large enough to rank as important features in the present-day scene. In the neighbourhood of Huddersfield there is a very prominent hill, Almondbury, seen from many miles around, the summit of which carries a hill fort of Brigantian origin. Between 56 B.C. and A.D. 43 the summit of the Castle Hill, as it was later called, was surrounded by two ditches and banks and for part of the way with a third ditch. Within this hill fort, Cartimandua, the queen of the Brigantes, had her citadel. After the defeat of the Brigantian leader, Venutius, in A.D. 74 the citadel was destroyed by fire, but of course the ramparts and ditches remained as they still are, a monument in the landscape. The site was again used between the eleventh and thirteenth centuries but with no modifying effect on the massive profile of the hill with its ramparts.[5]

When the threat of Roman attack was closing in upon the Brigantes, other large defensive earthworks were made, some of which are still objects of wonder to the traveller. Around Aberford and fringing a British kingdom of Elmet there are still the Becca Banks, a ditch and bank, two and a half miles long, the ditch in places twenty-five feet deep. Other sections of this complex group of 'banks' are about two miles long, and the whole forms only a part of what may have been defences of Elmet or a check to possible movement of the Romans against the north. Roman Rig,

[5] W. J. Varley, *Report of Excavations: Castle Hill, Almondbury, Excavation Committee*, 1939.

from the river Aire near Swillington Bridge to Scholes near Barwick in Elmet, is nearly 8000 yards long, and Roman Ridge from Sheffield to Mexborough, by Wentworth, a ridge up to nine feet high, is four miles long. Other works of comparable size were made in Wharfedale—the stone fort on Gregory and the vast entrenchment of the Ta Dyke, forty feet deep in parts, across the head of Coverdale, in connection with the same attack against which the Becca Banks were intended. These, however striking in themselves have to be looked for and are no longer more than minor detail in the landscape, although for 1000 years they were prominent enough to be re-used as important mediaeval and later boundaries.

The first big man-made feature which is still a part of our landscape is the network of Roman roads. Of these one from south to north is still followed by our most important road, A1, which in most of its course is maintained on Roman foundations. This road was of great interest and use to the Anglian invaders in the sixth and seventh centuries and through many later periods. It led clearly through the forest on a safe track, it crossed the mouth of all the dales and many settlements were located near to its line. Ecclesiastical parishes used the road as their boundary; it was the eventual link with the capital; along it military, political, and secular traffic flowed for well over a 1000 years. Very little of the Roman towns and buildings can now be seen except by the archaeologist, but this monument to Roman skill is traversed by thousands daily who benefit unwittingly by its presence.

It is true, however, to say that until the sixth century there were in the landscape only a few isolated monuments created by man, none of them large enough to have any real impact on more than a very limited scene. With the sixth century the invasions of the Anglo-Saxon and the Scandinavian people initiated changes and imposed a pattern which is still a widespread and basic element of our countryside everywhere familiar and taken for granted. It was this invasion through its many stages that created nearly all the villages we know today, laid down eventually the boundaries of parishes and gave us most of the names which spread over our maps. Three groups of folk, Angles, Danes, and Norse, in turn contributed to this settlement and today we can distinguish their contributions by a study of place-names, village patterns, and dialects.[6]

The traces of the Celtic folk 'Britons', who preceded Angles, are not very abundant except in the names of some of our rivers such as the Wharfe, Nidd, Calder, Don, Dove, and Went, with a few other minor stream names. There are a few areas where British names remain, one around Doncaster and Sheffield where Rossington, Ecclesall, and Penistone are among them, another in the British kingdom of Elmet where Leeds, Ilkley, Chevin and others are British names. None of the areas have any special feature other than the names and the few monuments already mentioned. A few names, Bretton, Wales, Walton among them, show that at those places the invading Angles found small pockets of surviving British natives.

The activity of the Angles in clearing woodland is evidenced by the abundance of place-names ending in *-ley* (leah = a wood or a clearing in a wood) and probably names ending in *-field*, like Sheffield, Dronfield, and Threshfield. These early settlers came up the Humber and penetrating by its tributaries spread into the Riding east of the watershed. Their villages are found along the riversides in close succession through the dales, and spread outwards across the plain in a close-set chequer. There was an expansion from the first settlements which probably date from the early seventh century when later generations went out

[6] A. H. Smith, 'Place names of the West Riding of Yorkshire', *English Place Name Society*, XXX–XXXVII, 1963.

to find farms of their own, farms now marked by hamlets or villages with a name ending in -*ton* (tun = farmstead). By the early ninth century the countryside in the lowlands and in all the valleys except those in the north-west was settled very much in its present pattern of villages and hamlets. Forest was now cleared around hundreds of villages which were laid out on plans which still persist to be recognised in many of them. Arable farming was widespread, more so than today, and many churches had been established, e.g. Ripon, Otley, Dewsbury, Doncaster.

A landscape of villages with arable fields closely enfolding them, set in an overall cover of surrounding woodland was evolving. The wood was being thinned by the demands for timber for building, for fuel and for fencing. The attack of grazing animals was sufficient to prevent any major regeneration of the woodland. Tracks from village to village were trodden out and a few older tracks, prehistoric or Roman, along useful lines were given a new life. There were as yet few large centres of population and no towns. The landscape was one of very numerous small villages.

In parts of the Riding the Anglian farmers have left a permanent mark on the land which they ploughed. They brought with them a heavy plough which was pulled by eight oxen driven in tandem. On level ground the use of this plough was simple but where fields were cleared in the narrow limestone dales where the fell sides slope down almost to the river alluvium, the only area available for extensive ploughing lay on the sloping ground rising to the foot of the first scar. To try to plough on this land with an eight ox plough was to encounter trouble. In ploughing along the contour of the sloping ground the plough tail would swing down the slope and a contour furrow would be impossible to make. Partly by plough and partly by excavation and fill, flights of terraces were built up, narrow but level and long, along the hill side. On these terraces the plough could be used effectively and sometimes, if the slope was long from foot to top, the plough could be pulled at right angles to the contours directly up and down the slope. These plough terraces were very permanent and are the *lynchets* which form a striking element in much of the dales scene. If we look at Malham village at the head of Airedale, a typical Craven village, we see the houses clustering round a village green and on each side of a beck. The east field of the village, is on the steep ground falling to Malham Beck but the west field lies on uneven, but less steep ground, between Malham Beck and a tributary.

As we look across the beck to the east field the lynchets dominate the view, the greater part of the visible field being covered by them. Field walls of the eighteenth century are in many cases built along the edge of a lynchet or round a group and those which cross the lynchets show a splendid profile of the rise and tread of the stepped terraces. In plan the lynchets are seen to lie in distinct and separate groups of three or four or more to a group. The lynchets of different groups may vary greatly in length and width, these being related only to the slope and extent of the ground. In a village commonfield the lynchets are not likely to be the oldest part of the field. The first problems of new settlers were to get land ploughed out and sown down on every nearest bit of level ground and to get their huts and the sheds for cattle in good order before labour could be spared for the big job of extending the commonfields. In fact the job of getting lynchets started was one which had to wait until all other aspects of the life of the village were assured. The contention that lynchets are solely the result of plough-ing in one direction is untenable on the steep lands of the northern valleys—the initial plough furrows could not have been made—some construction was inevitable even if subsequent ploughing promoted the intensification of the lynchets.

The lyncheted fields are almost confined to the limestone soils where in addition to simplifying the ploughing they helped to conserve the lighter soils from erosion by the swift run-off experienced in areas of high rainfall and steep slopes. In all the Anglian area of the limestone dales of Craven, lynchets are common to almost every village, but on the gritstone areas they are extremely rare. Occasionally a small flight is seen on some isolated hillside and one is tempted to think of these as the work of an individual who moved from a lyncheted area and made the experiment on his new ground.

The network of villages that the Anglo-Danish settlers formed on the lowland is the basis of our present countryside pattern. The villages started as small single farms or small community groups with a clearing around them in which their arable fields were made. These were fairly symmetrical so that the villages with their lands tended to form a very regular pattern and each village or township became a multangular patch fitting in with all the others and are generally of approximately the same size. Around the fields there was an area of remaining forest in which pastures were formed, glades in which sheep and cattle could graze. It was only in a few cases that there was any open land which could be appropriated as a common from the beginning. Roads radiated from the villages into the fields and in time footpaths from one place to another settled themselves roughly along the edge of the belt of fields and on the no-man's-land between townships. Except for the much greater amount of forest and the smallness of the villages, mostly only hamlets as yet, the map would, in the very rural areas, have a recognisable affinity with a map of today.

After little more than a century of peace the country was disrupted by Danish pirates attacking the east coast and then spreading inland with an invading army. York was captured in 867 and the conquest of Northumbria followed. However, in 876 peace was arranged and Danes scattered themselves among the Angles and made new villages, usually with a name terminating either in *-by* (a farm) or *-thorpe* (outlying farm or hamlet). After the stress of invasion this was a peaceful infilling which completed an almost continuous cover of villages over the lowland and the valleys there being a marked concentration around York and Doncaster. There was no significant difference in the way of life and thought of Danes and Angles. In fact Danish hamlets were often located within Anglian village territory, giving us the numerous double townships, such as Stirton with Thoralby, Winterburn with Flasby, and so on, in which the Danes had been allowed to make their hamlet in a corner of the abundant territory of the Anglian host village. Where the Danes did make a new village of their own in land not yet taken by the Angles, there was little except the name to distinguish it.[7]

During the settlement of the Anglian villages the Christian Church was established, though not without many vicissitudes. When the Danes settled they found church villages, which they named *Kirkby* (kirk, -by) and the distribution of these Kirkby names helps us to recognise the spread of the early Church. There is another indication of the pre-Conquest churches, however, which is of considerable importance as remaining in visible evidence, though hardly of 'landscape' dimensions—that is the very numerous Anglo-Danish sculptured crosses.

The first missionary preachers wandered around the villages carrying a wooden 'cross' staff which they set up where they preached, but they were centred for this work on Church communities, the early 'minsters' from which they covered a very wide district. Ripon was one such early

[7] The village plan and organisation were essentially like the Anglian; see A. H. Smith, *op. cit*. Introduction.

church which in the seventh century became the see of Bishop Wilfrid. Another early minster was established at Doncaster. Other churches, often built by local overlords or growing up round a famous hermitage such as Dewsbury, had graveyards in which stone cross monuments were erected. These churches became the centres of very extensive parishes of this period, as we shall see later. There are many churches where the remains of several such crosses still persist, often fragmentary but sometimes almost complete. Dewsbury, Otley, Ilkley have fine examples and many churches have portions of cross heads or shafts now preserved in the porch or vestry. We may take churches with a collection of Anglo-Danish sculpture as being on the site of pre-Norman churches.[8]

The tenth century saw another migration into our area, this time coming mainly from the west. In the ninth and early tenth centuries adventurous Norsemen had rounded Scotland, settled in the Faroes, Iceland, and the Orkneys, and had reached northern Ireland. By the tenth century these Vikings were making raids on the coasts of Cheshire, Lancashire, and Cumberland and soon pressed on across the Pennines to York which was captured in 919 by Vikings coming up the Humber, and held until 954. Their presence on the countryside is recognised by many words which occur in place names: *-thorpe*, (a secondary settlement), *-scale* (a sheiling), *-gill*, *-beck*, *-fell*, and many other words describing the natural features. This settlement was less widespread, more localised than that of the Anglo-Danish folk. There were large groups around Doncaster and York, but the strongest was in the north-west of the Riding; Settle, Malham Moor, Garsdale, and Dent were in this stream.

In the north-west there are few Anglo-Danish names except in the actual dales and they are generally below about

[8] W. G. Collingwood, *Northumbrian Crosses of the pre-Norman age*, 1927.

800 feet. On the high ground most of the names are Norse or Norse-Irish. There are very few nucleated settlements, the farms being spread along the hillsides and on the fringes of the moors, in a wide scatter with no focal point. This is admirably seen in Garsdale and Dentdale and in fact in almost every part of the north-west, where this distribution makes a strong contrast with the pattern of nucleated villages and hamlets in the lowland areas.

Let us look at three areas, each typical of a particular pattern which has a wide distribution. First, the Chapelry of Cowgill in Dent parish, is completely typical of Dentdale and Garsdale and most of the dominantly Norse area in the north-west part of the Riding, the part known as Ewecross wapentake (Fig. 3). The valley of the Dee here is narrow and steep sided and rises rapidly to a very extensive moorland common. The enclosed land forms a narrow zone on each side of the river, made up of small and extremely irregular fields running along the lower slopes. The zone of enclosed land is rarely half a mile in width, then above it comes rough pasture, enclosed in much larger allotments with ruled-line walls during the nineteenth century, and then again above that, the moorlands. The houses, mostly farms, are scattered in ones, and an occasional two, in a fairly even spread, two or three hundred yards apart. Nowhere is there a nucleus of houses. The place now counted as the centre lies at the junction of a principal tributary to the Dee, Cowgill Beck, where a Quaker meeting house, and one or two cottages form Lea Yeat, and the road changes from one side of the river to the other. The fairly recent church is quarter of a mile down the valley. This dispersion of houses and farm buildings over the whole area of lower land is a typically Norse valley settlement; on higher ground, like Malham Moor, the houses are widely scattered each in its own little enclave of enclosures, separated from its neighbours by the moor (Plate 4).

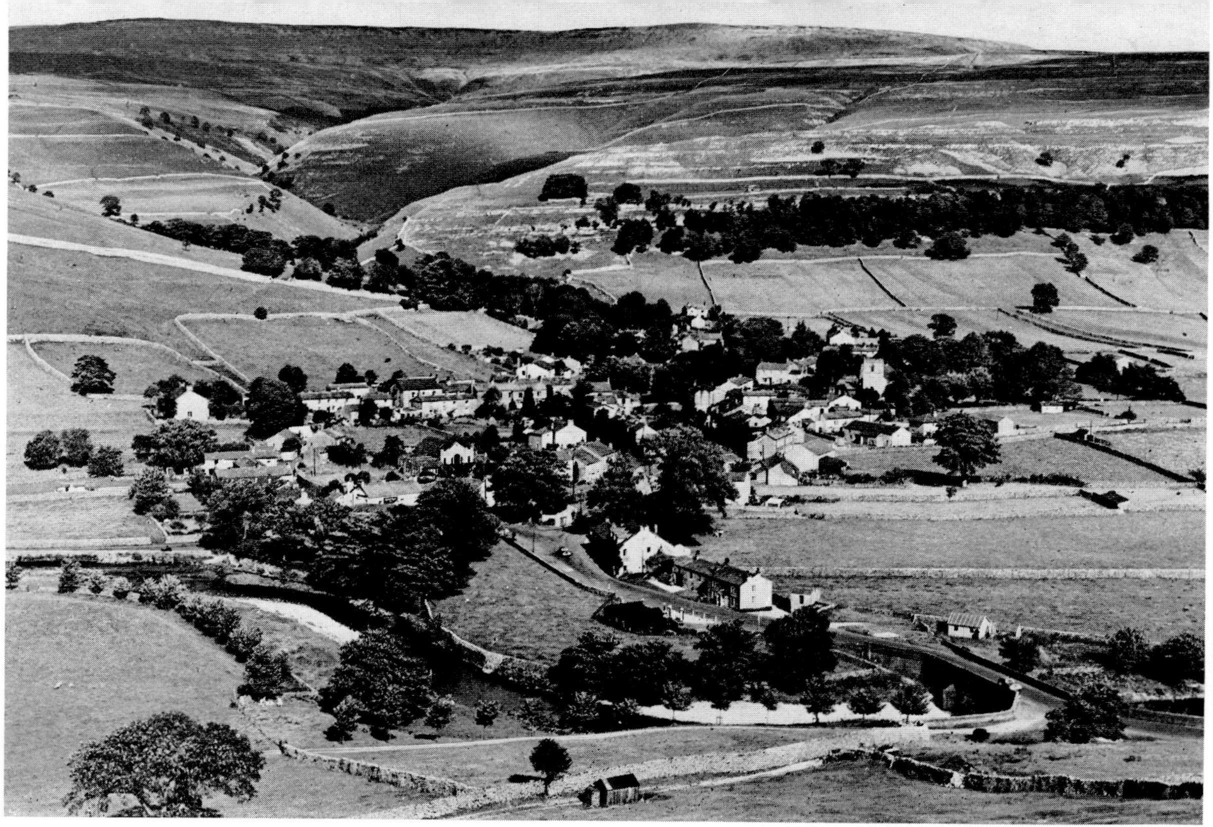

Plate 5 Kettlewell, Wharfedale. This shows the zoning—riverside meadows—town fields—scar woods—common pastures—moors.

Bertram Unne

C. H. W

Plate 6 Wharfedale from Netherside; Kilnsey, a grange of
Fountains Abbey is on the left of the glacial lake which was
drained in part by servants of the Abbey. This was a sheep
grange and is still important sheep country.

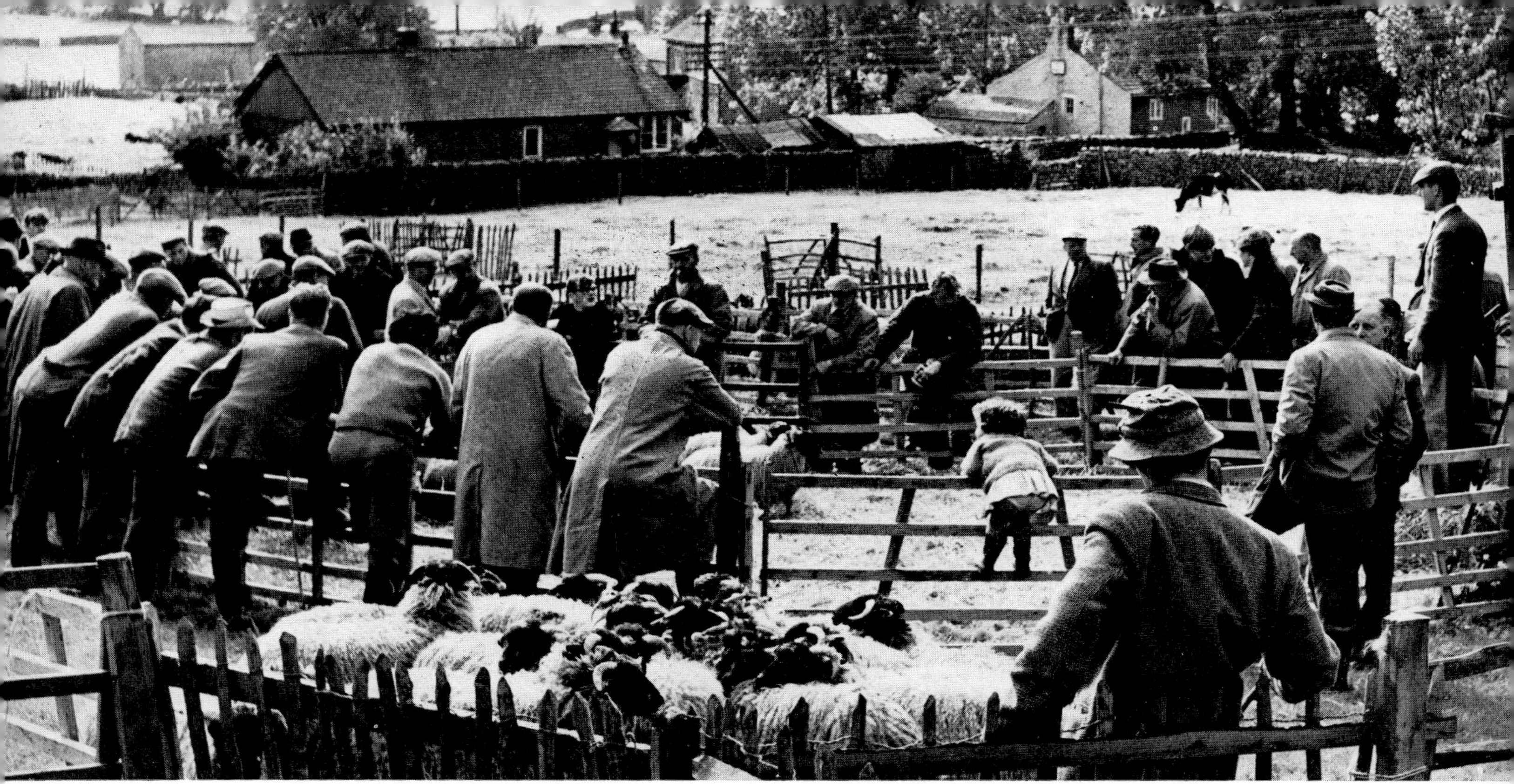

Plate 7 Sheep sale at Malham on a site where Bolton Priory gathered their sheep 800 years ago.

Bertram Unne

Plate 8 Wuthering Heights, Haworth. A moorland 'intake' now reverting to moorland. Notice the remains of small fields now invaded by heather.

G. D. Bolton

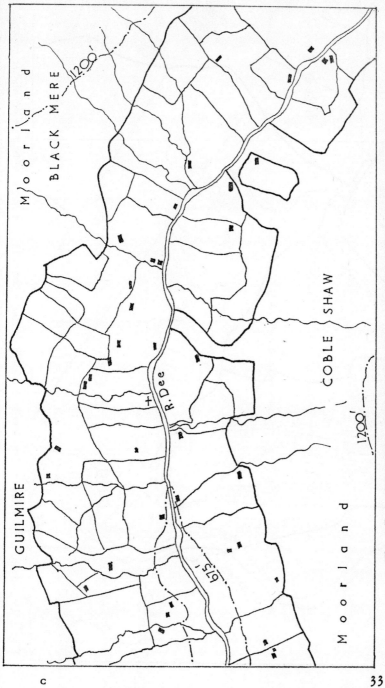

Fig. 3. Part of Cowgill and Kirthwaite; a Norse township with scattered homesteads.

GUILMIRE

Moorland

BLACK MERE

1200'

COBLE SHAW

1200'

Moorland

R. Dee

675'

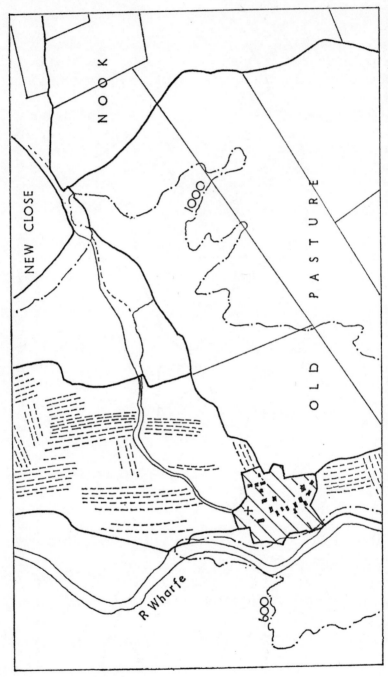

Fig. 4. Conistone; an Anglian nucleated village with lyncheted town fields and common pasture on higher ground.

NOOK

NEW CLOSE

OLD PASTURE

R Wharfe

1000

600

A contrast with this is found in the dales where the villages are Anglian. The villages are approximately at two to three mile intervals up the dale, each is a compact settlement and there are few isolated buildings between them. At Conistone in Wharfedale (Fig. 4) a large, eastward-running valley into which the Angles came by way of Humber and Ouse, the flood lands of the valley floor are meadow at about 600 feet and a narrow strip of rising land up to the foot of the first limestone scars is divided into a lower arable zone, where the fields have abundant lynchets, then a belt of closes and small enclosures going up to the scar foot. Above the scar, the edge of which is a few feet above 1000 feet, there is a long slope of pasture land forming the common pastures up to about 1500 feet, then the moorland above that. All the farms are congregated in a small village about mid-way of the township along the valley, and there are no other houses but these. The village had its two open fields, north field and south field, enclosed by agreement (see Chapter 3) before 1700. There is a scatter of barns or laithes in the crofts, and above the south field, the common *Old Pasture* starts at once outside the crofts. This zoned village, meadows, arable, pastures and moor is characteristic of most of the dales (Plate 5).

The third example is that of a township on the lower part of the coalfield, where the ground has a gentle uniform slope to the east, from the high ridge at 550 feet down to the lowest part about 300 feet. Near the centre of a township about two and a half miles diameter, there is the village of Woolley, again an Anglian settlement but typical of the lowlands (Fig. 5). The village is an approximate square, openly spaced, with the church and hall not far from the centre. In the seventh century the old hall, Wheatley Hall.[9] was superseded by a new and handsome mansion, Woolley

[9] It is to be regretted that the Hall has been demolished since this was written to make room for prefabricated farm buildings.

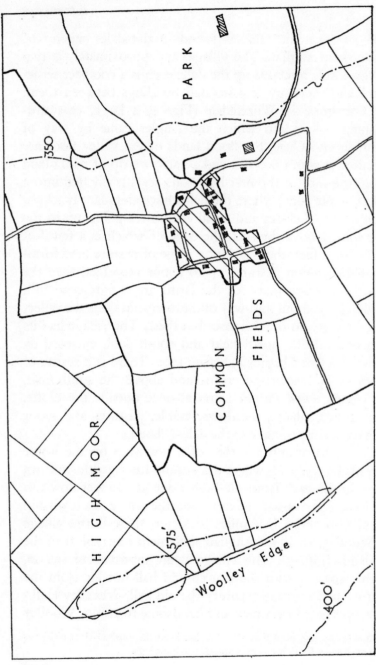

Fig. 5. Woolley; an Anglian village on the Coal Measures between Wakefield and Barnsley. Common near-circular plan; central village, fields, common.

Hall, set in a great park enclosed out of the lower and eastern part of the township. The open fields lay on the remaining three sides of the village, with, on the higher ground, an area of rough pasture called High Moor, not so great an area as the open fields. A narrow belt of moorland separates Woolley from its neighbouring villages. This in general terms is the plan of most townships in this part.

The village plans with their houses and fields as shown on the diagrams, which are based upon tithe surveys of about 1840, are not a true reflection of the state of the townships in the eleventh or twelfth centuries. While the original tofts and crofts form the nucleus there was some growth of the villages in the thirteenth to fifteenth centuries, and a few new farms have later helped to fill in the pattern. Yet in all essentials, these plans which have been carefully checked by field work, demonstrate something of the original disposition of housing, fields, and commons, and are sufficient to show conclusively the difference one finds in areas of different peoples and differing topography. In the case of Woolley during the last few years, because of its nearness to Wakefield and other large towns, there has been a great deal of infilling by new housing, dormitory accommodation for townsfolk. Wheatley Hall has been pulled down to make room for new building, and the later Woolley Hall is now an Adult College. Cowgill and Conistone are little changed with very little new building to be found in them.

There are of course many exceptions to these generalised township plans—some which originated as assarts within forest areas and others which have been won by reclamation from the marshes. Actual village plans will be discussed later but broadly speaking, the scattered, non-nucleated communities are characteristic of the predominantly Norse settlement, in contrast with the nucleated villages of the Anglo-Danish areas.

None of these settlements should be pictured as being made once for all, at a particular date, by an invading mass of folk. The settlement was not completed in the first generation when the groups involved were probably not larger than a family group or at most nine or ten comrades and their families. These cleared sufficient land for one or two farms and began the long and strenuous task of a wider clearance and recovery of land that was to last for many generations. Succeeding generations built more farms and helped to break out more land until young folk moved out of the growing village to find a new place for themselves in the still unoccupied land. This process of proliferation of hamlets, expansion of old ones and founding of new, went on for a few centuries and the general pattern of villages which we now know was probably not arrived at much before the eleventh century.

A major change in the organisation and government of the villages, though not in their shape and appearance, was made by the Normans who conquered the country in 1066. The complex network of feudal overlords, the multiplicity of manors, honours, fiefs and other new subdivisions and groupings of villages, with all the weight of feudal services, would have created havoc for the present-day historian if he had not had the vast record of the Domesday Survey. This survey of 1086–7 with its listings of manors, ploughlands, woodland, and meadow, with other miscellaneous information, gives a picture of the country as it then was. This was essentially a survey of the enormous changes of land ownership since 1066, a vast undertaking; and the briefest study of it shows that the method of recording was not uniform over the whole country. The more the record is studied the greater are the problems of interpretation posed by it. This is particularly true of the northern fringe areas where a too literal acceptance of the Survey leads into positions which create more difficulties than they solve.

None the less the Domesday Survey is a splendid document and the picture which it offers cannot in any way be ignored.

The form of the Domesday record is by no means the same over the whole Riding, and a landscape reconstructed only from that record will not be a picture of the true landscape at that date. None the less, the general results must be accepted as far as they go, and something added to them for completeness. In the area of the Coal Measures and down the Magnesian Limestone scarp, a majority of the vills are recorded with an extent of woodland which is stated in general measure of length and breadth. These records are sufficiently numerous to show that the Domesday landscape was well wooded in this part of the county. There is also an area of woodland in the lower Wharfe valley where almost every vill has woodland recorded for it and where the woodland extends westward to include the old forest of Elmet. There is no woodland recorded to the west of this except in the lower dales of the Aire, Wharfe, and Nidd. Meadow was present in many of the vills on and to the east of the Magnesian Limestone, and a small amount in mid-Wharfedale around Otley, but again, none to the west of this. The vills named in the survey cover practically the whole Riding, extending even up to Sedbergh in the extreme north-west, and to the upper part of most of the dales.

The blank areas are few but significant. In the east of the Riding the areas of the Humberhead marshes and the marshes near Thorne are empty of settlement, and this only reflects the emptiness of the Anglo-Danish settlement. In the north-west, however, the dales of Garsdale and Dentdale, the Rawthey and much of upper Ribblesdale are empty of vills, although this is an area rich in Norse settlement. These are single farms or tiny family groupings, not in the form of the Anglian villages, and are mostly on the higher land. They were ignored by the Domesday Survey, not being regarded as vills.

A view that is unacceptable is that put forward recently by H. C. Darby and I. S. Maxwell, that all the north-western part of the Riding was totally uninhabited.[10] In their maps of the Domesday Population they write across all this area from mid-Airedale and mid-Wharfedale right up to the county boundary the single word NIL, and in their map of uninhabited vills, they show not a single inhabited vill anywhere in all this vast area. This is surely a reflection only of the way the recording was done. We know that information was collected or given by reeves or bailiffs of wapentakes and by inhabitants. If the area of their totally uninhabited vills is examined carefully it will be seen to coincide very closely indeed with the wapentakes of Ewecross and Staincliffe, and in the case of Staincliffe boundary to have, as for example in Wharfedale near Ilkley and Addingham, plenty of inhabited vills on and close to the east side and nothing at all on the west, the Staincliffe side, in identical land and within a couple of miles. I do not believe that William's army worked, in their wasting, to the map of the wapentakes, and worked so accurately.

Similar criticism applies to the wasting of the area. This bears a similar close relation to the wapentakes, but also, great areas of the uninhabited vills are not recorded as waste. Over all the area said by some historians to be totally devastated, uninhabited and waste, the form of the entries in the Survey are uniformly of the following form. In the King's land in Craven, the form is:

"In Chersintone [Grassington] Gamelbar three carucates for geld
"In Freschefelt [Threshfield] Gamelbar four carucates for geld."

And so on through a long list of manors, then:

[10] H. C. Darby and I. S. Maxwell, *Domesday Geography of the North of England,* 1962.

"Manor. In Bodeltone [Bolton in Craven] Earl Edwin had six carucates of land for geld."

This followed by details of berewicks and soke, to the final summary, "Together for geld, seventy-seven carucates. They are waste." This, however, is only the total for the Bolton manor, and in the remaining more than fifty carucates there is no statement that "this is waste". In most of Craven the only form of entry is:

"In —— Gamelbar, three carucates for geld".

This is a common form in other parts, particularly of the King's land, where ploughs are mentioned in addition, where a value is sometimes stated, but where there is no mention of population.

This is not the place to enter into a long discussion of the form of the Domesday record, but these facts do encourage us to query the ideas which would be given by acceptance of the Domesday Survey without the supplement which local knowledge can offer.

We must then see the West Riding about 1086 as a countryside well settled with a network of villages most of which are still here today, set in a countryside of farmland, with a good deal of woodland in the part on the eastern foothills and to the east of the Pennines. On the very low eastern border of the county there was a wide area of marshes and fen with only a few villages on the sandy islands within the fen. In the Pennine Dales, there was a regular pattern of villages with their fields in the valley bottom, with pasture and woodland climbing up the fellsides towards the broad expanses of moorland, still unenclosed and wild or 'waste'. As one goes further west and particularly into the wapentakes of Ewecross and Staincliffe, then the uplands begin to be populated by Norse shepherds, their 'setts' well spread among the rugged uplands to all the features of which they had already given Norse names. We cannot believe that all population was absent from the Anglian villages of the dales, nor that they had been destroyed by the harrying of the North. This devastation may have stretched across the county along the line of the Roman roads, but the north-west country was far too wild and remote and unknown for the soldiers of William's hard beset army, suffering from the weather and the scarcity of food, to waste time on destroying tiny villages.

The valley bottoms still had the remnant glacial lakes and swamps, and woodland and forest was widespread.

BIBLIOGRAPHY

Chadwick, N. K. *Celt and Saxon*, Cambridge, 1962.
Collingwood, R. G. and Myers, J. N. L. *Roman Britain and the English Settlements*, Oxford, 1936.
Galbraith, V. H. 'The making of Domesday Book', *Eng. Hist. Review*, LVII, 1942.
Reaney, P. H. *Origin of English Place Names,* London, 1960.
Stenton, F. *Anglo-Saxon England,* Oxford, 1947.

2. The growth of villages and towns

Mediaeval scene, village plans. Forest areas. Monastic settlements. The early churches.

WE HAVE SEEN a fairly orderly pattern of villages arising in the dales and on the lowlands, in which the strongest influence moulding the plan of the village and its territory was the traditional agriculture of the Angles and Danes. The village as a collection of buildings, houses, barns, housing for stock and so on, was usually 'arranged' at least in part in a way that fitted the needs of this traditional agriculture. The most natural and widely accepted form of settlement in a new land is that which sets waggons, temporary shelters or maybe hovels, around an enclosed area within which there is a measure of protection from wild beast or other marauder, for the animals which must be contained and kept at hand. The substitution of more permanent and abundant buildings for the shelters of the first settlement, and the steady clearance of woodland as the fields were made and extended, improved the protective arrangement which increased in convenience even if the need for protection decreased. Thus we get 'enclosed' villages which can have more than one general pattern but which share the features of a central area which in time may become the village 'green', and which lies near the mid-point of their territory.

It may be an over-simplification to make anything like a rigid classification and say there are 'green' villages and 'street' villages, in which the houses and buildings are arranged around a green or along a road, with a few other shapes and definite types. We surely need to think of villages evolving and growing towards the many patterns we now have, and to assume that there was less differentiation in the earlier years. Few if any villages retain their original plan—all have grown and may or may not have been stabilised at some later date. The task of the field worker is to trace as much as possible of that growth and to recognise the causes which have brought about the present form of the village.

There is no doubt that many of the very regular square greens, with houses and buildings almost symmetrically placed around them, with 'back lanes' behind the tofts and between the village and the crofts, owe something to the original shaping of the village, but far more often they represent a sixteenth or seventeenth century tidying up of a ragged plan. The great rebuilding of those centuries and the tidy-mindedness of the eighteenth century helped to formalise our greens. The 'green' villages probably adhere to something like their earliest plan, but there must have been a long period during which this regular form was being approached. The first small cluster of hovels was bound to grow in numbers over the years—infilling and compaction of the tofts could well have been accompanied by an expansion of the central areas as stock increased. It is not improbable that the skeleton of the present plan of some of our more formalised villages was not arrived at until the quieter centuries between the Conquest and the Black Death, and was the product of many generations of progressive alterations.

The long double row of buildings with an elongated green between them, usually with a road along and continuing beyond the green may have been built originally alongside an older trackway, but except in the case of the few Roman roads, this is most unlikely. The earlier tracks generally avoid the lower ground, keep to the hillsides or to the gravel areas above flood level. When villages had begun on gravels and drier ground their linkage was often a feature which grew with the growth of a wider organisation. Once a road had gone among the houses then most later development would lie alongside it, and what had been a small cluster of houses could grow by stages into a longer and longer village, in which it is not very difficult by careful analysis to find the earlier part and to recognise later houses and clusters along the roadside and even later infilling between them.

The village of Flockton in south Yorkshire is seven miles from Wakefield to the south-west; the name suggests that this was a tiny settlement, Floki's farmstead. Among its present local names there are Flockton Mill, Common End, Flockton Moor, Flockton Hall, Flockton Gate, Pinfold Lane, Windmill Hill, and many others, but few of these names are earlier than the sixteenth or seventeenth century in their first recording. The village now stretches for a little more than a mile approximately east and west from Flockton Green at the east to Palace Farm at the west end, with most of the housing aligned along the south side of the road which is now the A637, a part of the road from Barnsley to Brighouse[1] (Fig. 6). Flockton Green is a more expanded part at the east end where a road forks north-east from the Barnsley road and the Green is built in and around the fork. This present mile-long village can be seen to have four distinct sections, both by its plan and by the buildings. Flockton Green is near the Manor House and the oldest remaining houses are along the road at the west end of this group which together is called the Green, where there is still part of a sixteenth century timber framed building to be seen. Other buildings have seventeenth century window mullions and other recognisable early fragments. The group of houses stretching north-eastward as far as Green Head

[1] O.S. 6 inches to 1 mile, sheets SE 21NW and 21SW.

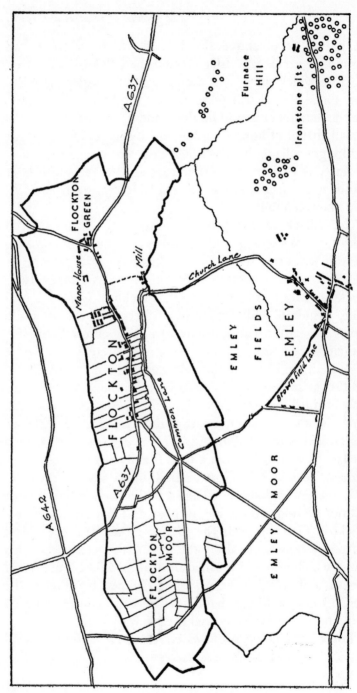

Fig. 6. Flockton and Emley; bank furnace and ironstone pits.

on the Hardcastle Lane contains other fragments of older structures, but in the fork and on what must formerly have been the triangular open village green, there is a 'fold' or 'square' of late eighteenth century buildings which was a hand-loom weavers' colony as late as 1820.

Half a mile to the west beyond the extent of Flockton Green there is the graveyard with foundations of the old church (the newer church which replaced it in 1869 is just across the road on the north side). The church seems to be near the beginning of the older part of the village with several groups of three or four houses to the west of it which are built at right angles to the road on its south side, many of which retain pieces of seventeenth century work and some which may be earlier. There is a fine school building with a date stone, 1668, and an old public house with many older features about its structure. From these groups of houses long crofts stretch down the hill slope to Flockton Beck which runs from west to east roughly parallel to the village and not more than a few hundred yards away. It appears that the groups of houses were extensions down the side of original crofts, and as the older fragments now remain in the lower buildings which are nearly all outhouses, it is likely that the houses against the road, most of them with Georgian improvements or rebuilding, represent the original dwellings with their tofts and crofts. The church path to Kirkby, a monastic grange site, half a mile away, but in the next parish of Emley, passes from the old church by Common End on the beck side, a seventeenth century farm with a small cluster of nineteenth century houses and cottages round it. Common Lane, running west from Common End goes across the now enclosed Flockton Moor. To the east Pinfold Lane keeps near the beck side to Flockton Mill, at the foot of Mill Lane coming down from Flockton Green. Between the Mill and Common End, the open fields of the village can be traced if looked for with care, lying between the village and the stream. The fields which lay to the north of the road are completely obscured by colliery workings and late development, but traces remain in the names.

To the west of the old part just described there are a number of houses and small groups, mainly of the late eighteenth and nineteenth centuries, which form an extension of the village, while the long stretch between Flockton Green and Old Flockton, called the Hill Top, is now almost continuously filled in with rows of small houses built in the late nineteenth and early twentieth century in connection with the local collieries. At present the village of Flockton presents a mile-long 'one street' village, but analysis has suggested that old Flockton and a later daughter-hamlet Flockton Green, have been extended and linked as the iron working and collieries developed and that old Flockton is probably a good example of a long or 'street' village, Flockton Green an example of a 'green' village, and the rest a typical industrial infilling.

The more we look with care at the villages of the West Riding the more obvious it becomes that we are seeing everywhere the results of the reaction of the early settlers to a new topographic environment in which they looked for certain minimum *desiderata* for the continuance of their customary agriculture. The abundant variation in topography from the flat, rich-soil plains of the vales of York and Trent, to the narrow valley floors of the upper Pennine valleys with steep, even precipitous, rocky slopes, and the marshes of glacial lakes still occupying most of the flat bottom lands, forced upon the Anglian settlers a degree of adaptation and compromise not demanded of them in the more uniform areas of the Midlands and East Anglia. Classifications arrived at in these more uniform parts call for more and more adaptations as they are pushed into the margins of the highland zone. None the less the tradition of a certain plan to which the village and its lands should conform remained strong and villages which fit closely into the 'traditional' pattern are found from time to time, even in the more remote of the Pennine valleys.

Arncliffe lies in Littondale,[2] three miles above its junction with Wharfedale. The river at Arncliffe bridge is at 720 feet O.D. and the fells rise on each side by a series of high limestone scars and terraces to moorlands reaching over 2000 feet O.D. A stream, Cowside Beck, runs down from Darnbrook Fell and Malham Moors, through a deep and very spectacular gorge-like valley and joins the Skirfare, the river of Littondale, at Arncliffe. This stream has built up a fairly large delta into what was a glacial lake in the main valley. The surface of the delta, a very flat cone, varies from 750 feet O.D. at its head in the mouth of the side valley, to its broad front along the river, a fall of about thirty feet, part of which is accommodated by a relatively steep front of about ten feet to the present river channel. The village of Arncliffe is well placed on the surface of this gravel delta, well above the flood levels of both stream and river, on ground sloping very gently to the east. The village green is a long oblong with a row of buildings, mostly houses with some farm buildings among them, set fairly close together, on each side parallel to the dale. Behind the buildings are small squarish crofts, roughly one to each building. The mill is on the Cowside Beck at the north end of the village and the church is on the high bank top near the river at the other end. A few buildings close each end of the green. A large Victorian house occupies the site of the earlier manor house at the south-west corner approach. The village has two common fields, to north and south between the river flats and the steep limestone scars, and in each there are traces of the rig and furrow ploughing prior to the enclosures. A series of extensive common

[2] O.S. 6 inches to 1 mile, sheet SD 975 W.

pastures are spread along the terraces of the limestone fells up to the base of the Millstone Grit heather moorlands. The whole plan is very recognisably that of the typical Anglian 'green' village, skilfully adapted to, and elongated along, the topography of this narrow mountain-sided valley.

By the fourteenth century a chequer-board pattern of evenly spaced villages, related in plan to two or three recognisable types of 'green' and 'street' villages, covered the central zone of the Riding, on the east creeping on to the edge of the Hatfield and Humber marshes, and on the west pressing into the Pennine dales. The Humber marshes, however, remained with few settlements beyond the occasional hut of fisher or fowler, while on the Pennines there were extensive areas of 'forest'. The term forest does not necessarily imply a large area of dense woodland growth but rather an area of wild land reserved for the king's hunting, within which such trees as existed were protected for the benefit of the deer and where sheep were not allowed to graze because, by grazing the saplings, they would have inhibited regeneration of the trees. Agriculture was very severely limited to small 'assarts', clearings made under licence and cultivated only for the needs of the forest servants and for some winter feed (beans) for the deer. The form of settlement in the forest was not in villages or even hamlets, but in 'lodges'. A lodge was usually one original dwelling to which a small group might attach in time. It would have no arable fields and only small garden-like assarts or an occasional croft. Most forest areas had a village on the edge which had been created to house the principal forest officers and these villages are usually post-Conquest, twelfth or thirteenth century and follow the general village plan with open fields and pasture. Buckden in Wharfedale is such a village.

The old forest of Langstroth and Litton in the heads of the Wharfe and Skirfare valleys had several lodges which by the fourteenth century had grown into small hamlets. These were all originally Norse farm settlements. Cray, Kirkgill, Raysgill, Yockenthwaite, Deepdale, Beckermonds, and Oughtershaw were listed in Langstroth in the early thirteenth century and by the end of the fifteenth three others had been added. These together now (*c.* 1500) had forty-three tenements. One lodge has disappeared and the others today have only one or two farms—none has grown into a village. In the Forest of Knaresborough and the Honours of Kirkby Malzeard and Ripon which together covered upper Nidderdale there were at the Domesday Survey eight manors. In the area, however, there were also ten other small Norse settlements of one or two houses, sheep farms with small assarts around them. In the twelfth century the upper dale was divided between Fountains and Byland abbeys though the hunting was reserved to the donors. Both abbeys created granges and farms on old and new sites so that in the early fifteenth century, in addition to the pre-Conquest settlements there were at least thirty more. All these new places are still to be seen (except one or two drowned in the reservoirs), but most of them are single farms and only a few, like Middlesmoor, have become tiny hamlets.

There is no specific character by which these farms are recognised beyond the names. The monastic cartularies must be read with care, and by map research many of the names, farms and properties can be recognised on the one-inch Ordnance Survey maps. These should then be checked on the six-inch map and an examination on the ground undertaken. In this work, field names, the existence of ancient walls, the general wall pattern and its relation to that of the wider area, may all give clues; the absence of tithe apportionment in the Tithe Awards made around 1836 to 1840 also assists in restoring a plan of the properties. Roads linking them with the parent monastery may sometimes be distinguished even if great lengths are now overlain by modern road. The surveys and rentals in the records of the Augmentation Office, now in the Public Record Office, are a rich mine of local detail as it was at the time of the dissolution.[3] This reconstruction of the monastic estates can be an exciting and rewarding pursuit.

Much was done by the monastic granges to establish these numerous sheep farms, to improve the upland pasture and, through the heavy grazing of their flocks, to clear the scrubby woodland.[4] Some of the great sheep walks which we have today, Malham Moor and the upland fells throughout the north-west of the Riding, we owe in part to this monastic colonisation and use (Plates 6 and 7). In the southern part of the Riding the sheep played a smaller part, the rich limestone pastures were absent and the Millstone Grit moorlands offered only very rough grazing.

None the less the monasteries left their mark on the landscape in other ways. While there was a little iron making in the Knaresborough Forest and other parts of the north-west, in the areas granted to the monasteries in the Calder and Colne valleys, iron working on a large and well organised scale was carried out by them. Bradley, near the junction of Colne and Calder, became an important grange of Fountains, almost entirely taken up in iron mining and making. Bentley Grange and others south of Wakefield and west of Barnsley, down through Cawthorne and towards Sheffield were all busy with the iron trade in which many monasteries, Byland and Rievaulx as well as more local ones shared. In many areas, and particularly clearly around Bentley and towards Emley and Flockton, the bell pits of the ironstone mines are still to be seen covering large areas

[3] The records known as Particulars for Grants, in the Public Record Office are also valuable for their topographic detail.

[4] A. Raistrick, *The role of the Cistercian Monasteries in the history of the Wool Trade in England*, Int. Wool Secretariat, 1953.

and the furnace sites are known and the structure of one or two remains intact. After the dissolution, these iron working sites became the foundation of the great south Yorkshire iron industry of the seventeenth and eighteenth centuries, based upon local ore and charcoal. In the making of iron vast quantities of charcoal were used and the monks did much to clear wooded ground over many parts of the Pennine slopes and at the same time make new land available for the expanding fields of the growing villages. Many of the fine woodlands in that part of the Riding owe their good condition to the coppicing introduced by the seventeenth century ironmasters.

In the Calder valley, in the vast and ancient parish of Halifax there was a scatter of small settlement that is different again from the general pattern, but has some similarity with the forest areas. Most of the upper Calder lay within the Manor of Wakefield or the Honour of Pontefract (the townships of Southowram, Elland and Greetland). The earls of Warren who held the manor of Wakefield made upper Calderdale their hunting area with the great fourteenth century park of Erringdene (still well marked) as the breeding ground for their deer. Such place names as Roebucks (a farm in Warley township), Buckstones, Doestones, Deerstones, Wolfstones, come from the days when this was a hunting forest. The courts of the manor for this area were held at Halifax, at the Moot, later the Moot Hall (only recently pulled down), and Halifax became the parish to which all Calderdale above Rastrick belonged. The parish is large, about twenty miles by twelve miles, part of the ancient Saxon parish of Dewsbury, and contained twenty-five townships. The valley bottom is very narrow and the valley sides very steep, so that most of the early settlements were made on the broad shelf where the top of the grit forms a wide belt of more gently sloping land. The movement of settlements into the valley bottoms, with the coming of industries, will be discussed in Chapter 6.

Many village names in this area contain the terminal element *-land* as in Elland, Soyland, Greetland, Norland and so on: this is combined in many cases with a Norse prefix, Nor-land, the north land; Greet-land and Stain-land the rocky or stony land, but the use of *-land* was continued in Middle English as settlements were won from the waste in post-Conquest times. Another place-name element which is very abundant is *-royd*, but this is largely attached to single farms, only rarely to a hamlet as in Mytholmroyd. *Royd* is post-Conquest and is derived from the English *-rod*, a woodland clearing or assart, and is usually attached to a descriptive term, e.g. Eckroyd, the oak clearing, Jackroyd, Jack's clearing, and so on through a very numerous and wide range. These names indicate a gradual settlement in isolated farms throughout the whole area of upper Calderdale, on the hillslopes up to above 1000 feet O.D. and they may range in date from the twelfth to the sixteenth century.[5]

Thus in the upper Calder there is a different pattern of settlement with a few villages, chiefly of 'street' type accompanied by a very wide scatter of individual farms and hamlets, assarted in the wilds of the vast area of the parish of Halifax. Halifax as the church town, the site of the manor courts and with an early and important market and fair, outstripped all other settlements and became an important mediaeval town, soon to develop even more as the centre of the woollen industry. Towns which were of comparable growth in the earlier post-Conquest centuries were the castle centres of Knaresborough, Skipton, and Pontefract, serving their respective Honours. The earls of Warren had Conisborough Castle from a few years after the Conquest, but also had Sandal Castle near Wakefield, and it was Wakefield which grew to be the chief mediaeval town, Conis-

[5] T. W. Hanson, *The Story of Halifax*, 1920.

borough remaining only a village. In the southern part of the Riding, the Norman family of de Busli had a grant of some fifty-eight manors and Roger de Busli built his castle at Tickhill, six and a half miles south of Doncaster and three and a half miles west of Bawtry. For much of the mediaeval period it was the important centre of Tickhill Honour which included all the country around Sheffield and along the southern border of the Riding, and it had an important market acting as a collecting station for goods coming to and from Bawtry, the port on the Idle, tributary of the Trent. The settlement of this area followed the pattern of the other lowland to the north of it, but to the west in the upper valley of the Don and its tributaries, settlement was very sparse and followed the pattern of the upper Calder valley.

Sheffield now one of the chief cities of the north, does not fit easily into the more formal village patterns, though a close study leaves no doubt of its original plan. Its site is in the junction of the upper Don and its tributary the Sheaf, where the Hallam ridge of high ground rises between them. This position lies at and rises from 500 feet O.D. on what is roughly the dividing line between the woods and moorlands of the Pennines to the west and the village and farmlands to the east. There was an Anglian settlement on the tip of this ridge near the river junction and in the twelfth century a small Norman castle was built, probably replacing the earlier hall. A village grew up along the crest of the ridge along a way which later became the High Street. One of the Town Fields was developed on the northern flank of the ridge from the street down to the banks of the Don, and a market and the church were located near the castle. A manorial mill and bridge over the Don were near the tip of the ridge. Across the Sheaf and east of the village was fairly open ground, a large area of which became Sheffield Park, only enclosed into small farms after 1700. This area is now entirely built up but still keeps the name of Sheffield

Park. Many names of streets and areas in the city preserve landmarks of the mediaeval village. A careful analysis of the street plan of the modern city can still reveal the layout of the older village and its fields. Castle Green, Castle Orchard, Ditch, Hill and Folds fill out the plan of the castle surrounds—Mill Lane and Pinfold Lane and a number of croft names are all pointers to the early plan. Other names worth a little thought are Water Lane, Green Lane, Camp Lane and other lanes now in the heart of the city. Pea Croft, Well Meadow, Moor Fields, Bell Fields are other clues to the plan of Sheffield as a village.

The present city has absorbed several villages and hamlets but the centre of most of them can still be found and the street plan shows stages in their amalgamation.[6] To the west of Sheffield the land rises quickly to the wild expanse of the Millstone Grit Midhope Moors which range between 1000 and 1800 feet above sea level. They are free of settlements and are penetrated by the deep gills of the upper Don. On the west these moors extend to the Derwent valley and the county boundary with Derbyshire runs for a long way down the centre of the Derwent river. This western fringe lies within the Peak National Park and its eastern side is ringed with reservoirs in every valley. Two settlements on this edge have grown to be important industrial towns, Penistone and Stockbridge.

Penistone, a pre-Conquest Village with a name containing a possible British element, remained a small village until the coming of the cloth trade, when it became a centre of cottage industry, a virtual outlier of the Colne valley textile area. It remained a small place until in the nineteenth century Cammel Lairds brought an overspill industry from Sheffield which completely overshadowed the textiles and created what was, in effect, a new steel town. For a time it

[6] A recent excellent study of such amalgamation with Sheffield is that by David Hay, *The village of Ecclesfield*, 1968.

was a small market town on the main road from Sheffield
to Huddersfield with fairs for horses and horned cattle. A
writer in the mid-nineteenth century just before the advent
of the steel industry says of it, "It is a small market town,
little superior to a village . . . noted for the number of moor
sheep sold at its market and fairs."

Stockbridge is strongly in contrast with Penistone, being
a nineteenth century township taken out of the very old
township and parish of Bradfield. It accommodated Sheffield overspill, and has a 'garden village' and an industry
almost entirely concerned with refractories for the Sheffield
steel plants. It is an important dormitory for Sheffield.
Apart from these two so different towns, the whole of this
western area has only a few scattered farm settlements, the
names of two of which, Cubley and Schole Hill, are indi-
cative of early cattle rearing (a clearing with cattle stall, and
a hill with a shieling, respectively). The other settlement-
names support the picture of thinly settled upland with
cattle herding on the moorland farms.

The earliest places to attain important status were the
castle towns which were the centres of the feudal government of large Honours. The large numbers of retainers,
and the regular traffic to and from the Honour courts made
them natural market centres and based the life of the town
on factors which changed very little for several centuries
(see Chapter 7). The centres of these towns usually have the
same features, the castle with the market usually not far
from the gate, the High Street and the church) a plan which
is soon seen, even today. The castles may have become
ruins in most places, but they are still there and are now
being excavated and revealed to the interested public. The
High Street and market place are still the commercial centre
of the town although shops and stalls have been replaced
by modern shops. There has been some infilling and some
enlargement of buildings but the basic plan and activity

of these old town centres has survived in a remarkable manner.

The pre-Conquest landscape was one of villages with no 'towns' in the sense in which we now use the word. By 1086, however, a few manors had emerged as the administrative centres of larger estates belonging to the king or the Archbishop of York. The king's estates included Knaresborough, Aldborough, and Wakefield. Ripon and Otley were manors of the Archbishop. One of these early 'towns' was Ripon, though its foundation was largely ecclesiastical. In 661 Eata, the abbot of Melrose, founded a college of monks there on ground given to them by King Alfred of Northumbria. After the disputes of the Synod of Whitby in 663, the monks left their place and Alfred gave their monastery and thirty tenements there to Wilfrid, then nominated as Archbishop of York. Wilfrid began the building of his church at Ripon. Eddius Stephanus says for the years 671–8, "St Wilfrid the bishop stood in front of the altar, and turning to the people in the presence of the kings, read out clearly a list of the lands which the kings for the good of their souls, had previously and on that very day as well, presented to him . . ." The list covers lands right across the county into Amounderness (now part of Lancashire), and Ripon thus became the ecclesiastical centre for a very large area. In 886 Alfred the Great incorporated Ripon with a Wakeman, twelve Elders and twenty-four assistants to govern it. At the Domesday Survey it was the holding of the Archbishop of York and had fourteen berewicks with forty-three carucates of land and thirty ploughs, as well as the soke of six other places with twenty-one and a half carucates of land and fifteen ploughs. This large estate of land and vills was the Liberty of St Wilfrid. The Archbishop of York also had the manor of Otley with about sixty carucates of land and thirty-five ploughs; there were sixteen berewicks to this manor so that Otley could well rank as a mediaeval town. The church and market place with a broad street dominate the town centre even today but the later expansion has been along the roads up and down the dale.

Of the king's manors Wakefield, Aldborough, and Knaresborough were of the size of small towns with sixty carucates of land and thirty ploughs, thirty-four carucates and eighteen ploughs, and forty-two carucates and twenty-four ploughs respectively, and all with berewicks and soke in numerous other vills. Tanshelf which later was incorporated in the newer town of Pontefract was in 1086 a town with sixty burgesses and forty other tenants, a church, and three mills. Dadesley, now represented only by a solitary farm and part of the castle town of Tickhill, had thirty-one burgesses and sixty-six other tenants, a church, and three mills, while Conisborough had an unusually large amount of land held by sokemen, but only a small amount of land in the vill.

These represent practically all the pre-Conquest places big enough to be called towns, and all but Conisborough developed after the Conquest into important castle or market towns. Some years after the Conquest Roger de Busli built his castle at Tickhill and a new borough town grew round it with an important market. Much of the territory of Tickhill extended into Nottinghamshire and its castle may have served as a guard to the southern entry into Yorkshire. In the years following the building of the castle Tickhill increased rapidly to be for a time probably the largest town in south Yorkshire. Its position on the roads north and south and from west Yorkshire to Bawtry, made it a commercial centre of importance, the residence of several merchants, but its importance began to decline in the fifteenth century. The remains of the castle, market cross, almshouses, and a mediaeval timbered building are still to be seen near the centre of the town.

Its neighbour, Bawtry, is a good example of the new

towns created after the Conquest, largely in response to increasing trade and population. It is first mentioned in a charter of 1199. In 1213 Robert de Vipont created a borough there with free burgesses and before long got a market charter and a fair for the new town. Bawtry is on the Great North Road about a mile north of its crossing of the river Ryton. The Idle, tributary of the Trent, is at the eastern side of the borough and is navigable and the town became at once a river port. There is a wide market place along the main road and the church is near the river. Much of the early plan is still visible. From the Poll Tax returns of 1379 Bawtry appears to have become already a busy town with several merchants and craftsmen, and it retained this character for many centuries.[7]

The increase in population and trade during the twelfth and thirteenth centuries led to the settlement of several new towns of which another is Boroughbridge. The old town of Burgh, later Aldborough, which we have already mentioned as a king's manor was related to the Roman roads leading to the north and to York and was located in the Roman town of Isurium. The event which brought about, or perhaps decided the location of the new settlement was the building of a new bridge over the Ure which is mentioned in 1145. The town of Burgh became Aldborough (Old Town) and the new town near the bridge-head and on the border of the old town fields, was Boroughbridge. Much of the plan of this new town is still traceable. Three mills belonging to the lord were alongside the bridge. The bridge was at the head of navigation on the Ouse and Ure, and for many centuries lead and other commodities from west and north Yorkshire were shipped at Boroughbridge for York or Hull. From 1179 to 1183 the Pipe Rolls contain many references to lead being sent from *ponte de Burc* to Selby or York for transhipment to London or abroad and this shipment from Boroughbridge

[7] M. Beresford, *New Towns of the Middle Ages*, 1967.

continued through several centuries. The new town of Boroughbridge grew slowly, but by the beginning of the fourteenth century it had increased and was a thriving place.

Pontefract started as the castle town of the de Lacys. The castle, built on a rocky prominence about the end of the eleventh century with a keep added in the mid-thirteenth, was one of the most impressive in Yorkshire. The town lay west of the castle with a central Micklegate, wide enough to serve as the market place. Two other streets, North Street and South Street were roughly parallel one on each side of it. It is likely that Pontefract was the name given when, the castle was built adjacent to a pre-Conquest village, Tanshelf, which at the Domesday Survey was a king's manor with sixty burgesses. The old village stood not far from the fords over the river Aire and the Roman road running north and south, and when it was granted to Ilbert de Lacy it was inevitable that he should build his castle on the nearby rock and make a town as the centre of his large fee. In the thirteenth century the town and population had grown and a second borough was created as an extension to the west of the castle town. This emphasises the new prosperity by the size of its market area, now largely built over but traceable by the street names— Market Place, Wool Market, Beast Fair, Salter Row, Shoe Market Street, Corn Market, etc. The new borough had the name of West Cheap, again indicating a market, and received its charter between 1255 and 1258.

BIBLIOGRAPHY

Hunter Blair, A. P. *Introduction to Anglo-Saxon England*, Cambridge, 1956.
Deansley, M. *The pre-Conquest Church in England*, London, 1962.

Knowles, M. D. *The Monastic Orders in England*, Cambridge, 1941.
—— *The Religious Orders in England*, Cambridge, 1948.
Power, E. *The Wool Trade in Mediaeval English History*, Oxford, 1941.
Powicke, M. *The Thirteenth Century*, Oxford, 1953.
Tait, J. *The Mediaeval English Borough*, Manchester, 1936.
Thirsk, J. *Peasant Farming*.

3. Enclosure landscapes

Industrial areas 'intake', etc. Parliamentary enclosure.

ENCLOSURE LANDSCAPES dominate all the lowland scene but the multiple pattern of walls and hedges is now so much taken for granted that any appreciable area on which walls or hedges, however few, are not to be seen at once arrests the attention. To most folk such unenclosed ground appears to be bare, wild, and lacking the marks of civilisation. On the level land of the east of the Riding, an intricacy of hedges sits everywhere outside towns and villages, stretched over the countryside like a net with a slightly uneven mesh. One is tempted to see areas of mesh-enveloped land rather than a pattern of fields laid edge to edge—the hedges seem to dominate and to leave the land to a secondary and merely background position. This feeling may, however, be the reaction of a person brought up among the country of dry-stone walls where the overlaid pattern is drawn in much finer and less exuberant lines, so that one is easily conscious of a territory on which a fine pattern has been etched. In the Pennine area the pattern of enclosure has a striking difference from the near-overall coverage in the lowland. The hills seem to have thrust up through the close net, leaving it undamaged in the valley bottoms and on the base of the steep slopes, but above this the mid-slopes have stretched the net to a far wider mesh: finally on the summits only an occasional single thread remains crossing the highest moors.

From the crowded walls of the valley bottom other walls climb the hillsides and become attenuated at the edge of the

63

moorland. Yet over most of the Pennines long walls stretch
out like antennae across the moors and over the water-
sheds from this edge of the enclosures, demanding attention
as they go up-the hills apparently ignoring steep and crag
alike, ruling their straight unbroken line across a wild
topography.[1]

The wide expanses of moors above Haworth, stretch
for many miles of heather where they are traversed by deep,
precipitous stream courses, diversified with patches of
threatening bog flowered with cotton grass, and with the
dark lowering crags of the Millstone Grit. Nevertheless,
except on the highest summits they are humanised by the
derelict farms. There are only a few places on these moors
where one can get out of sight of at least one and often
several, of these old homesteads. The farmhouse is hardly
more than a large cottage sturdily built in the solid grit
of the moors, continuous under one roof with its barn and
shippon, making a long low group of dark grey building
(Plate 8) blending into the scene. These farms are often
marked by the solitary bullace tree or perhaps a rowan,
or one or two sycamores planted near the buildings. A
complex of three or four small fields or crofts now surrounds
them defined by broken-down walls and a subtle, though
slight, change in the moorland vegetation which has returned to recapture them. Although the buildings may be
unroofed and their walls ragged and broken and the field
fences are more gap than wall, their presence in the moor is
an unconscious assurance that folk have lived and worked
here, that the wild to that extent has once been tamed. The
Howgill Fells in the north-west of the Riding, with their
smooth slopes unbroken by wall or hedge, and unmarked
by ruins, appear like velvet-clad mountains from some new
land. To turn from the close-walled valley sides of the dales
to such a group of fells, is to realise how essential a part of

[1] A. Raistrick, *The Story of the Pennine Walls*, Clapham, 1967.

Bertram Unne

Plate 9 Markenfield Hall, near Ripon. A fourteenth century moated Hall, now a farm.

Bertram Unne

Plate 10   Hopton Old Hall, upper Hopton, near Mirfield.

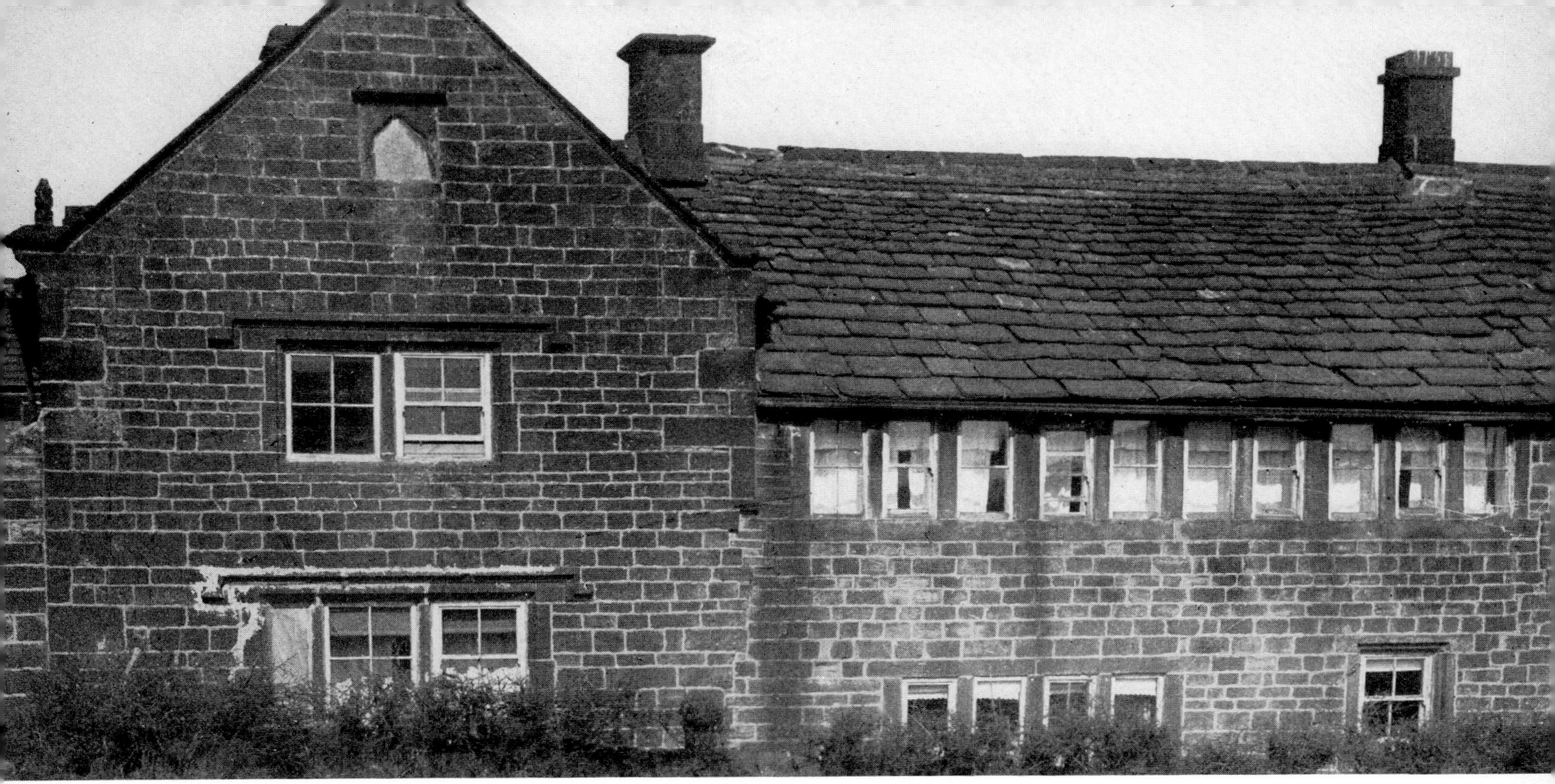

Plate 11 Weaver's house near Penistone. The long ten-light window on the first floor formerly lighted a row of hand looms set against it. *Author*

C. H. Wood

Plate 12 Temple Newsam, Leeds, *c.* 1630; in grounds which were landscaped in the eighteenth century. Now a Leeds Museum and Park.

the scene enclosure walls and hedges have become, and how much we miss them where we can no longer take them for granted.

It has been the continuing habit of man from the earliest times to enclose for his use and safety some small section of the wild, so we can expect enclosures to be of many ages and degrees of sophistication. The progress of enclosure has almost always proceeded by addition—more ground taken in from the waste—a constant accretion on the edges. We might then without presumption look for a great range in age and some change in the character of the enclosures which have an ancient village at their centre, as we move from centre to periphery, as we move outward both in space and time. Size and shape, structure and even the material used in them might well be expected to show differences diagnostic of different ages. None the less the common needs of populations in a similar environment are likely to lead to comparable patterns of enclosure and indeed this assumption is amply justified when enclosures over a wide enough area are studied in detail.

A wide survey soon assures us that patterns of settlement and of enclosure fall into a relatively few general types which have specific features so that we can indeed, apart from minor local variants, speak of 'patterns' as something tangible and real. When patterns can be dated in particular examples they show an agreement of date within fairly narrow limits, sufficiently so as to justify their use as a means of dating approximately the stages in the growth of a settlement.

Most of our villages are of pre-Conquest origin and where they have escaped urbanisation there is often a recognisable nucleus of the early settlement, a group of homesteads around some central space or along a track side, to be detected on the map and verified on the ground. Although no original buildings will remain for inspection

E

the pattern of small enclosures, in spite of modifications, may still be very evident. The basic unit of the village, the *toft and croft*, the piece of land on which the first shelter or hovel was built (toft) and a small enclosure (the croft) big enough for a garden or enough to pasture an animal, sometimes half an acre in extent, sometimes more or less, had a remarkable permanence. The original house will have been replaced many times—wattle and daub giving way to timber, timber to brick or stone, and a roof of branches replaced by thatch, then by tile, slate, or stone; the style of building advances and accommodation changes and improves, but toft and croft remain as the permanent recognisable unit, changing little over the centuries.

There is an innate desire in most of us for a place of privacy, a small area which is ours to shape and use to our own desires and fancies—the clearly divided, well-fenced 'back gardens' of our countless modern estates, with the small 'front garden' public to the highway, these so essential features of modern housing whether detached or 'semi', are only the instinctive respect for croft and toft that has survived more than a dozen centuries of nucleated settlement.

Whether the original boundaries of toft and croft were marked with hurdles, ditch and bank, hedge, fence, or stone walls built with land clearance stones, their lines were fixed—deviation could only be made by trespass on to a neighbour's land or encroachment on to the common field or highway. The area of the croft was too small to suffer much by divided inheritance and the toft was the minimum room for a house which when large enough might be divided into 'east end' and 'west end' to accommodate the family of an inheriting son and his widowed mother, or a brother, but subdivision of the house could scarcely go beyond this.

If we could have seen a village soon after the Conquest,

or if by our researches we can recognise and recover its plan by map and field work, we would almost certainly see the houses, tofts, and crofts, placed as a group fairly symmetrically near the centre of the two or three common fields. The heart of the village, the tofts with their dwellings clustering around the central space, is wrapped round with the protective girdle of crofts, and narrow ways creep through this zone to the fields outside. In a fairly common plan the tofts face each other across a space and the crofts extend behind them. Before the Norman Conquest the open fields had been under plough for two or three centuries and were fenced from the surrounding pasture. A fence is still to be seen occasionally marked by a few ancient thorn trees, *x*-generation replacements of the originals, on a decayed bank with a ditch on the outside, and embracing what had been the tofts and crofts and ploughland. Outside this lay the wild and wood in the glades of which sheep, cattle, and pigs found grazing. In the areas where stone walls were used this outside fence of the original fields is often made with huge land-clearance boulders in its base and is often very irregular in its line. It has been easier to move the line of the wall to include very large boulders than to move the boulders merely to get a straight line. Built as they are, on a very broad base, these old walls tend to be pyramidal in section, no 'through' stones to bind them, and using all sizes and shapes of stones just as they came on the ground. This first boundary enclosing the fields is often clearly seen on the six-inch maps, recognised by its nearly complete circumscription of the village and by its irregularity and continuity.

This picture for the village and its field within its enclosing bank could serve for most of the vills listed in the Domesday Survey. The ones in the lowland on richer soils might have half a dozen or up to ten carucates while those in the dales and the foothills of the Pennines were commonly smaller with only two or three carucates for taxation. Between the eleventh and thirteenth centuries the population increased and such returns of land and holdings as *Kirkby's Inquest* and the Feudal levies reveal that most villages had nearly doubled their area of fields or even more than that in some cases, between the Domesday Survey in the mid-eleventh and these surveys of the late thirteenth century.[2] This added land lay on the periphery of the original village, a ring of added clearance taken from the waste or occasionally a whole new field added at a convenient part of the old plan. Again in the fourteenth and fifteenth centuries the fields tend to be stabilised and substantial boundaries mark the completed second generation of enclosure.

Looking on the ground or the map for these early enclosures, crofts and fields, we must forgo the modern idea of regularity, that a wall or fence must be straight, that areas must be laid out tidily on a drawing board and built walls and fences made to right lines. The first enclosures were made in an uncultivated area—the pressing need was for a fence or wall to enclose stock and keep out the wild animals of the surrounding forest. Advantage was taken of every natural feature, rocky outcrop and large boulder; areas were not measured by the surveyor but taken by eye and by guess, chosen by the need of the moment, and the result is the tangle of roughly equal but irregular little enclosures which fill the old part of a village. By the time later enclosures of the open fields are made, the plough team had ruled out a pattern for the new fences which gives a uniformity never found among the earlier ones.

We can look at a village plan which has had very little growth since the eighteenth century and in which the stages of enclosure are still well shown on the maps and clearly seen on the ground. If we take Linton in Craven, it

---

[2] *Kirkby's Inquest for Yorkshire* is printed as Vol. 49 of the Surtees Society.

lies in upper Wharfedale and is quite typical of many villages in the dales. The township of Linton is one of the four
which together make up the ecclesiastical parish of Linton.
Its lands extend from the bank of the river Wharfe over
rising ground to the moors which are heather clad and
which are still rough grazing common, with some shooting
over them. At the Domesday Survey in 1086 the land was
recorded as two carucates, in these parts the equivalent of
about 150 acres, as the carucate seems to have been between
about sixty and ninety acres. It was part of a large area of
manors held by king's thegns.

The village is roughly square surrounding a green with
the Linton beck running across it. The present houses,
mostly of seventeenth century structure, lie on the east
and west sides of the green, with eighteenth century almshouses on the south side, and a plantation occupying the
position, on the north side, of more seventeenth century
houses which were pulled down about 150 years ago. The
crofts in which the houses stand can be recognised around
the dwellings, and they extend outward to a very massive,
irregular wall separating them from the town fields. On the
east and west sides of the village there is a large area of
fields surrounded by a wall which is not very straight in any
part, and which continues right round the group of fields.
The cross-walls within the enclosed area abut against the
old wall but never cross it and do not join the line of any
walls which abut on the opposite side. These are walls that
by land clearance have at some time replaced the first
hedges or fences of the earliest recognisable town fields
which would be cultivated in open field strips and furlongs.

These two enclosures (Fig. 7) are respectively seventy and
seventy-two acres, and, allowing for some slight intrusion
of gardens beyond the original area of crofts, these might
quite well be the representatives of the first town fields,
estimated in 1086 as being of two carucates. In *Kirkby's*

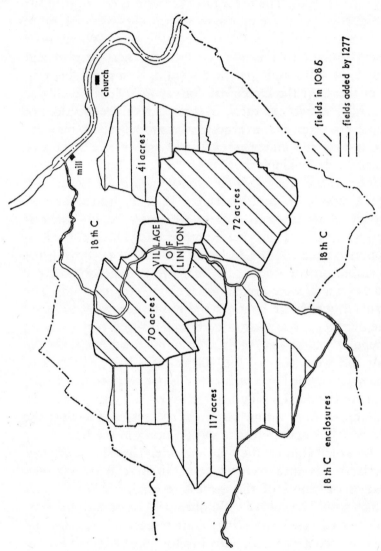

church

mill

41 acres

72 acres

VILLAGE OF LINTON

70 acres

18 th C

18 th C

117 acres

18 th C enclosures

fields in 1086

fields added by 1277

Fig. 7. Linton village and its town fields.

Inquest of 1285, Linton was returned as being of four carucates, or doubled in size. This was by the addition of more fields, and on the ground as well as on the map, we can see two more ancient walls against which cross walls abut in the same way as that just described. The field to the west of the village is on good, fairly level ground and is approximately 117 acres, while that on the east is on ground rapidly falling to the river, and is forty-one acres approximately. Together these make very nearly 160 acres, again roughly two carucates of eighty acres, a very average figure for this district. Among these four fields there are some areas of lynchets in those of the first pre-1086 enclosures and in the two others there are many areas of rig and furrow ploughing with the reversed-S shape, and so presumably mediaeval.

Nearly all these fields had been subdivided by enclosure by agreement or by the exchange of strips before the end of the eighteenth century and only a few small patches of open field remained within them in 1793.

A change in the open field agriculture had been fore-shadowed even in the thirteenth and early fourteenth centuries when some of the monastic tenants with grants of land within a manorial town field had sought and obtained licence to lay strips together, presumably by exchanges such as Ranulf son of Ulf de Otterburn granted to the monks of Fountains Abbey. "Moreover he has exchanged with them a certain part of his land and the land of his men living in Malham namely acre for acre so that their [the monks'] cultures shall be together in the same field separate from the grantor's and the borganes and waste and rocky places lying between the lands which he has exchanged with them they shall make into cultivated land, to their profit, as best they may." This is only one of many similar exchanges of 'acres' or strips granted so that lands or acres might lie together. In the fifteenth and sixteenth centuries this creation of fields by the exchange of strips had been common particularly where the enfranchisement of copyholders to freeholders was taking place. In manors like Conistone and Hebden and many others which had been sold by their lord to the whole body of tenants who then became freeholders, there was, during the seventeenth century in particular, a considerable buying and selling of 'doles', 'selions', 'lands', 'acres', all of them open field strips, by whatever name they are specified, until the more substantial freeholders had gathered together and created enclosed fields and closes. In a survey of Malham in the opening of the eighteenth century the map has still a large, walled field, roughly rectangular, the property of one owner, and called Ingber, being within and about one third of a larger field 'Open Ingber' which was still held by many owners in separate strips.

In Grassington several dispersed strip holdings in the open fields were sold about 1605 and the new owners at once began a process of selling or exchanging them, often with an adjustment in money to equalise the values, and sometimes with a provision for making a wall. The result of many of these sales was that the west open field was transformed into a series of long parallel walled enclosures of varying width, but all showing the typical shape of the plough rigs from which they had been accumulated. This can be seen on Fig. 8, where the present fields in the group depicted all have the name 'Mains', with an owner's name added to differentiate them, and all have the slight reversed-S-shape typical of mediaeval plough rigs. Where such a pattern is seen on a map—and the six inches to one mile is a useful scale for this kind of 'spotting'—an examination of ground will often confirm the map deductions by revealing plough rigs on some of the fields. Spring, with the new young grass and a low sunlight, offers the best conditions for this work.

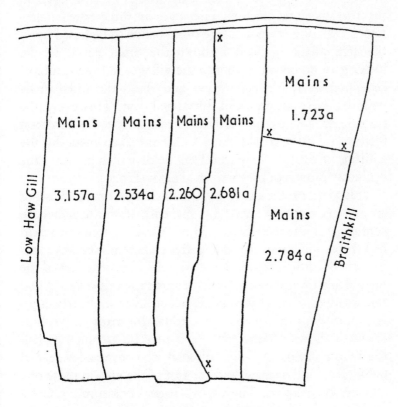

X X two recent subdivision walls

Fig. 8. Mains field, Grassington, enclosed by sale and exchange of strips, 1610–1720.

If a whole township can be mapped in this way the pattern of the mediaeval open fields can often be recovered, in which the rigs are clustered in groups or furlongs and the furlongs are grouped into two or three town fields. Lanes radiating from a village often prove to be based upon the access lanes to and through the town fields. In the lower ground off the Pennines the villages in the main have remained in arable cultivation and these rig and furrow patterns have often been ploughed out. However, the pattern of hedges and ditches often shows the common features of early enclosures which have been made by the addition of strip to strip into long fields which preserve the outlines of much of the mediaeval fields (Fig. 9).

This type of enclosure by the exchange or purchase of strips was well advanced by the end of the seventeenth century and was usually carried out until a whole town field had been enclosed. In the early eighteenth century the process of enclosure was often completed for the rest of the open fields by agreement, when a surveyor was called in and the area was divided into fields which were more rectangular, unrelated to the plough strips. In many townships the map shows a large section, it may be as much as half the whole township fields, divided into reversed-S-shaped fields, long and narrow, and the rest of the area in more of a chequer-board plan. The change to an enclosure by agreement was generally done to speed up the process. The exchanging of strips could and often did go on for several generations, and until it was completed it could leave awkwardly isolated strips among the new fields. As the pressure for enclosure increased, the desirability of a quicker process, and the emergence of the surveyor as a professional man to be hired, made the new procedure possible and attractive.

Among the Parliamentary Enclosure Acts which we shall be discussing later all but a very few are first and foremost

Fig. 9. Clifton near Dewsbury. Enclosure by agreement.

concerned with the enclosure of waste, moors and common pastures. In the 386 Awards for the West Riding which are available for study in various repositories, less than twenty are enclosures of open field only—more than 250 are for open field, commons, pasture and waste and in most of these the open field is only a small area left from enclosures by agreement, and brought into the Act to tidy up and finish off a process that had been going on for generations.[3]

The Linton Enclosure Award of 1793 was made for "several open and uninclosed fields called Low Field, Kelbottom, South Field, Langriggs, Forelands and other small fields which be intermixed and undivided . . . 50 acres, and also a certain Stinted Pasture called Linton Pasture . . . 480 acres." The moor beyond the Linton Pasture was left unenclosed, and the better ground outside the four fields we have already discussed between them and the township boundary, which was an area of no great extent, was walled into a few large fields soon after the enclosure award. The walls of the 1793 award stand out on the map by their geometric arrangements with precisely ruled lines and the approach of their enclosures to strict geometric quadrilaterals with only three L-shaped fields among them, given that shape so as to reach a stream for cattle-watering.

The Linton pattern is repeated in most of the dales townships—the adjoining townships of Burnsall and Threshfield, for instance, got an Act to enclose 1690 acres of common and pasture and only seventy acres of open field; Conistone and Kettlewell, 8000 acres of commons and pasture and 150 acres of open field: and an extreme case perhaps, in the same dale, Appletreewick, 6330 acres of pasture and common and only nine acres of open fields. These small areas are all that remained of the open fields, the rest being already enclosed by agreement.

[3] National Register of Archives, *West Riding Enclosure Awards*, B.A. English (Ed.), W. R. (North Section) Committee, 1965.

Alongside the break-up of the manorial pattern of common field cultivation, the pasture was subjected to a more careful scrutiny. The monasteries had helped to establish wool production as a profitable industry and the demands from a growing cloth trade were being felt. Pasture for sheep was taking on a new significance and as the importance of arable land declined in the upland areas so pasture acquired a new value. There was a definite movement to improve common pastures by enclosure and by the regulation or 'stinting' of the number of animals using them. This was easy in the townships where the freeholders were also lords of the manor, or in those where the lord could find an increase of income through such enclosures. In Conistone the Old Pasture had been enclosed at an early date in the twelfth century as a practical measure to limit the stock from wandering over wastes which extended over many square miles of very rough upland. With the growth of the township and an increased interest in wool, pastures were enclosed from the commons and waste, the New Close in 1587, Nook and Kelber in 1629 and Bycliffe about 1650. In all these the freeholders of the manor agreed to pasture animals in numbers proportional to the ancient rent formerly charged on their tenements. The total 'stint' or 'gates' varied from time to time, between thirty and forty horses in Kelber, 1200 to 1700 sheep in New Close, 130 to 150 sheep and some beasts in Nook, and 130 to 200 beasts in the Old Pasture.

The effect of such enclosures of common pasture is seen in a pattern very common to most of the dales townships, where a zone of now enclosed 'open fields' around a village is followed by two or three enclosed common pastures, outside and above which lie the moors or commons. The enclosed pastures are generally large and well defined natural areas still easily recognised by their natural feature boundaries in spite of the subsequent partition into smaller enclosures.

Another type of enclosure was most common in the growing textile area of the Calder valley with its many tributaries, an area largely covered by the ancient parish of Halifax. Within the many townships the enfranchisement of copyholders to freeholders had gone on steadily, alongside an increase in the population. Outside the common pastures lay wide moorlands which were the waste of the manor, on which both copyholders and freeholders claimed rights and privileges, pasture for sheep, turbary, getting stone for building and repairs, and other small rights. On the 'waste' it was recognised that the lord of the manor had some right of enclosure and this he exercised by granting to many of his tenants licence to make small enclosures on which he could levy a fine on entry and a small annual rent, the total of which over the great areas which he controlled, formed a welcome addition to his resources.

During the sixteenth century the lords of the manors granted many such enclosures on the waste so that in 1589 it was reported that almost a quarter of the copyholders of Halifax had recent enclosures on the waste, of which only the more useless parts were now left. Early in the century it had been said of Halifax that "the manor . . . conteyneth, with the buyldinges in the townes and manors 5338 acres, 2042 acres whereof is enclosed, 500 acres granted to be enclosed, and the rest common and unenclosed upon which copyhould is reserved."[4] In 1604, sixty-two people in Northowram had made enclosures from the waste and in 1633 it is reported by the Justices that many houses had been built on these small enclosures. Opposition grew, however, as the waste was reduced more and more and the rights of pasture, turbary, and other common rights were rapidly diminished. In 1615 the twenty freeholders of

[4] Leeds Public Library, TH/HX/B4/4. Rental of Halifax Manor, n.d. but early sixteenth century.

Langfield complained to the court that of 900 acres of waste more than half had been enclosed and only the worst and useless part was left for the exercise of their rights of turbary and pasture. The court ruled that no further enclosure of the waste and common could be made by the lord without the consent of the freeholders.

In the sixteenth century there was a remarkable increase in population in the upland areas. The 'Halifax Act' (2 & 3 Philip & Mary, c. 13), 1555, says, speaking of the woollen industry in the Halifax district, "By means of which industrye the barreyn Groundes in thos partes be nowe muche inhabited & above fyve hundrethe Householdes ther newly increased within theis fourtye yeares past." The threat to the wool drivers threatened these new inhabitants with poverty. In 1587 the township of Grindleton in the manor of Slaidburn in Bowland, petitioned to be allowed to enclose part of their commons, because the town "is of Late greatly increased in Buildings and dwelling-houses and thereby much more populated than heretofore it hathe bene, by reason whereof the Auncient groundes used and imploied to pasture medowe and Tillage are in no sort able or sufficient to mainteine our said ffree-holders and copieholders whereby muche povertie dothe dalie encrease emongst them...".[5]

The effect on the landscape of the enclosure of the waste was that over a large part of the textile area where most of the town fields have long ago been obliterated by building, the upper slopes of the valleys and the edges of the moorland are covered with a continuous area of small fields, generally rectangular and between one and three acres in extent. The pattern is strikingly uniform on the ground between about 800 and 1100 feet above sea level. There are houses scattered among the fields, one to every five or six

[5] P.R.O., Duchy of Lancaster, Warrants and Commissions to Survey, Bdle. 12.

enclosures and these are roughly contemporary or very little later and are mostly late seventeenth and eighteenth century houses generally with a barn and shippon built under the same roof. These houses with the group of fields round them make the small 'hill farms' many of which are still viable, producing milk, eggs and poultry for the neighbouring industrial populations. Many are places where the man combines two occupations, part-time farmer and part-time mill worker.

The growth of population in the Pennine industrial areas was a great incentive to the production of grain on the more favourable lowlands. Open field land in the industrial valleys was turned more and more to pasture and food was brought into the area, at first by 'badgers' and then through markets of increasing importance. The seventeenth century saw a decided differentiation of occupational areas—food producing arable agriculture on the plain and cattle-rearing, milk, poultry and sheep on the upland.

On the lowlands of the Riding the pattern of enclosure was progressing toward increased arable area, the production of more grain and a reduction both of waste and common pasture to that minimum required for dairy purposes. The 'waste' was almost limited to coppice and plantations, or absorbed into the larger parks that were created in the seventeenth and eighteenth centuries. The enclosure, by agreement mainly, of the open fields before the eighteenth century has ensured that the pattern of many villages and their field boundaries have embalmed the mediaeval landscape in a recognisable form. Much of the traditional housing of the seventeenth and eighteenth century is still in use, and many of these villages have not grown much in size. This is particularly true on the area of the Magnesian Limestone and the country just east of it on the Triassic edge.

In the area of arable farming the enclosures in no serious

Plate 13 Threshfield Quarry (building stone and stone setts), about 1901. Old crane and a group of banker hands.

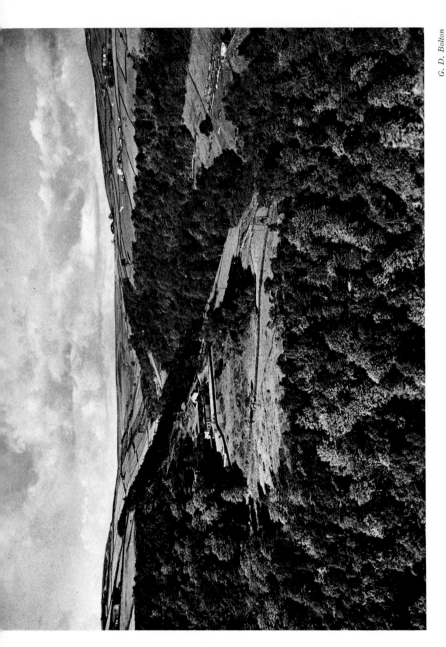

G. D. Bolton

Plate 14 Crimsworth Dene, a Millstone Grit valley. A popular beauty spot adjoining Hebden Bridge.

Bertram Unne

Plate 15 Magdale, near Honley. A valley in the heart of the heavy woollen district. Early mills are along the river-side.

Plate 16 Remains of lead-mining on Grassington Moor, Wharfedale. Mine hillocks are spread along the length of the Coalgrovehead vein.

way altered the manorial aspect of the countryside. The old villages remained, even if they increased a little in size, but their growth was limited by the little amount of new land which could be taken in within the relatively small township boundaries. The church, manor house, and in some case the newly created park of a wealthy landowner, remained as the principal features of the parish and the only additions were a few farms newly built on the enclosed pasture land, and a new road system. From the country round Ripon down to the country around Doncaster a striking feature of the landscape is the great number of small villages which remain not much larger than they were two centuries ago, and which still have many of their buildings in the old style, with very few new buildings to mar the general picture. In the concealed coalfield part of the Riding, these small villages have scattered among them the new villages, many of them even towns, created for the deep collieries that have been sunk mainly in the twentieth century.

Hooton Pagnell is fairly typical of many of the old villages, set in a proper rural countryside but within two miles of it having new colliery towns which have been built near to or around a tiny village nucleus. South Kirkby, South Elmsall, Ardwick le Street, and Thurnscoe are such colliery towns, of 8000 to 18,000 population but each coming to a clearly defined edge against the arable fields. Hooton Pagnell is a township or parish of only just under 2000 acres, seven miles north-north-west of Doncaster, and on the junction of the Magnesian Limestone and the Coal Measures, so that the eastern half of the parish is on the limestone and the western half on the shales of the coal measures. Its population was 246 in 1961, but in 1931 was 316. The village is central to the parish, a long street running north to south with a triangular village green, and at the south end the church and Hall. There is a pound and a village cross at the foot of the green. Near the northern boundary of the parish there is a small outlier called Moorhouse, with three farms and one or two cottages, while the village in 1931 had eight farms in it and many cottages. On the limestone ground there were three open fields, the North, East and South Fields, while most of the shale area on the west was commons and woods, much of them taken in at a very early date into small closes and enclosures.

The open fields were gradually enclosed by the exchange and later by the purchase of strips though this was not completed before the late nineteenth century. The field fences and the whole lay-out of the village and parish have a strong mediaeval flavour.[6]

The great belt of Parliamentary Enclosures that runs across England from east Yorkshire to the Dorset coast lies mainly to the east through Lincolnshire but its fringe covers the West Riding up to the Magnesian Limestone belt. Even here, however, the proportion of the open field enclosures was negligible. The most striking change in this eastern part of the Riding was due to the drainage and reclamation of the fens and marshes. This effort to control flooding and to reclaim land was extended over most of the lower courses of the Don and Thorne rivers. The large area known now as the Humberhead Marshes extends by the wastes of Goole Moors, Thorne Moors, Hatfield Moors and so to the Lincolnshire marshes around and south of the Isle of Axholme. Through all the early periods and to the Middle Ages this was largely open fen and peat moss, the territory of wild fowlers and fishers, almost devoid of settlements except on the few upstanding small islands of gravel or Keuper Marls, or the larger area of the Isle of Axholme. The whole area was less than twenty-five feet above sea level, and all was liable to severe flooding.

The recovery of this area started in the seventeenth

[6] A. G. Ruston and D. Witney, *Hooton Pagnell*, 1934.

century with the work of the Dutchman, Cornelius Vermuyden, brought over in 1626 to drain Hatfield Chase.[7] This was part of the marshes which had been created a chase for the hunting of deer and such animals as browse on the numerous patches of pasture and scrub on the islands. Vermuyden saw that much of the flooding was due to the restricted run-off of the rivers, particularly the Torne and Idle which wandered across the flat country in innumerable unstable channels towards the Trent. He cut new courses for these rivers which secured a quicker run-off and began the recovery of the land. A new course was cut for the Don from a low part of the river to the Aire between Snaith and Rawcliffe. The new course was only successful at the expense of the lower Aire. The additional water caused that river to back up and to create extensive flooding around Snaith. A second and better scheme was the so-called Dutch River which was taken from the Don at a mile and a half above its junction with the Aire and ran in a direct course to the Ouse at Goole. Besides reducing the flooding this new cut improved the navigation of the Don by cutting out several miles of difficult river passage which included the acute bends in the Ouse at Kilpin and the difficult entry to the Don from the Aire near Airmyn.

Between 1800 and 1860 much of the land was raised in level by warping. Drains with sluices allowed the silt-laden waters of the Ouse and Trent to flow over the land at high tide, and with the closing of the sluices this was held back to drain slowly back to the rivers during low tide, leaving behind a thin layer of alluvium. These layers gradually built up and many acres of peat mosses had been warped within three miles of the river Trent and much more had been improved by covering it with alluvium dug or

[7] S. Smiles, *Lives of the Engineers*, 1862, I, p. 36 ff., and G. Stovin, 'A Brief Account of the Draining of the Levells of Hatfield Chase', *Yorkshire Archaeological Journal*, 37, 1950, pp. 385–91.

dredged from other areas and channels. Some of this land reclamation had been paid for by the sale of peat cut from 3000 acres of Thorne Moss. The warped lands made excellent ground for potatoes and by the end of the century this part of Yorkshire with the adjacent parts of Lincolnshire became the most important potato-growing land in England.

The landscape created by all this work was one dissected by innumerable perfectly straight drains, cutting the land into parallel strips, sometimes miles in length. The drains had sluices, many with a tiny house for the sluice-keeper and in many places where levels were difficult, there were pumping stations. Many of the pumps were operated by a windmill, and some by a horse-mill. The landscape was a miniature Holland and the effect was increased by the presence of a proportion of Dutch settlers from the time of Vermuyden who had introduced a Dutch element into their building. A number of new farms was built on the reclaimed land, but no hamlets or villages were formed. The principal change in the nineteenth century was the substitution of steam for wind and horse power for the pumping, and in the twentieth century the bringing of electricity for this purpose. This is now a landscape of enclosure in which drains and canals take the place of hedges and enclosures are strictly laid out by the engineer, mathematical and rigid in their pattern.

BIBLIOGRAPHY

Beresford, M. *History on the Ground*, Lutterworth, 1957.
Gray, H. L. *English Field Systems,* Cambridge, Mass., 1915.
Orwin, C. S. *The Open Fields*, Oxford, 1938.
Tate, W. E. *The English Village Communities and the Enclosure Movements*, London, 1968.

4. Vernacular and secular building

Park landscape

THE AREA OF the West Riding is sufficiently large and its variations in climate, topography, and geology wide enough to secure that there is no one type of building, either in structure or materials, that could be picked out as being typical for the whole Riding. Even within such a relatively simple class of building as the peasant house, everywhere comparable in its function and minimum requirements, the incidence of available materials, timber, stone, brick, has so influenced the style of features and design that for any study it is essential to recognise again some of the basic divisions of the area. It is only in the houses of the wealthy, the larger halls and mansions, where the expense of bringing in materials from a distance was not a consideration, and where an architect was employed, that the fashion of the period and the taste of the client and architect dominate. These larger houses owe little to the locality where they are built and often show more conformity with houses of similar size almost anywhere in the country, than they do with anything local to them (Plate 9).

Shelter for his family and his animals has been contrived by man from the earliest times, so that although the vast bulk of building that helps to make the present landscape dates from the seventeenth and later centuries, there are a few buildings, either entire or only fragmentary, which survive from the earlier times. This is true of two groups but to a different extent. Monastic buildings, churches, and castles have in great measure survived, though often almost rebuilt in successive 'restorations', and some are still in use; of the second domestic group only foundations and occasionally a part incorporated in a later building are still to be seen. The two groups tend to be associated with different physical areas. The remains of the earlier peasant buildings are in the main preserved on the fells of the 'highland zone', that is the fells and dales of the Pennines. The other group consists of buildings essentially of the lowlands and plains of the eastern part of the Riding. Even in the case of parish churches the very large parishes with a great number of townships in each which are so characteristic of the highland zone, means that the older churches are few in number and very widely scattered and that there are many villages with no church or with a fairly modern, usually nineteenth century, 'chapel of ease'. In upper Airedale, the townships of Otterburn, Bell Busk, Winterburn, Calton, Airton, Scosthrop, Hanlith, Malham, and Malham Moor, all share the one church at Kirkby Malham —in upper Wharfedale twenty-nine townships share seven churches. The castles and abbeys tend to lie along the ground towards the Pennine foothills and only rare examples, Skipton Castle, Bolton Priory and Salley Abbey, are within the actual Pennine zone.

In the highland zone of the west and north-west, the domestic building began with the hut circles of the Bronze Age farmers, which in the Iron Age of the Romano-British, first to fourth century, were developed in large numbers, associated with areas of fields and sometimes grouped in clusters which for description have occasionally been spoken of as villages. These are all remains which are clear to the trained eye of the field worker and archaeologist but which otherwise make little impact on the countryside, most of them being unknown to the local population except perhaps as a collection of meaningless gravel banks.

As most of our villages date from the Anglo-Danish

settlement, the earliest structures we might still expect to recognise in the rare case of survival are those of the more substantial houses of pre-Conquest date. As the early methods of construction continued for several centuries, in some cases until the sixteenth or seventeeth, there are many examples of post-Conquest date which are still in their essentials, examples of this earlier building. The most radical change was the introduction of the rectangular planned house, generally with foundation layers of stone, and a house in which there was probably accommodation for some stock as well as the family.

The earliest structures in the villages were probably of timber and wattle only, hovels giving the minimum of shelter and to our eyes atrociously small. The one or two larger houses only, would be 'cruck' built. Such houses are on a rectangular plan, the main support for the roof being two or more, usually three or more, pairs of crucks, which are curved beams got by splitting a suitably curved branch or trunk of a tree lengthwise, so getting a symmetrical pair of timbers to be set up as an arch. The crucks were set up at about ten to sixteen feet apart forming a 'bay' or unit, with the cruck feet spread to about ten or twelve feet. At about six to eight feet from the ground a cross piece was set across each cruck, morticed and pegged into the cruck members, giving an approximately A-shaped frame. The ends of these cross members extended beyond the side of the sloping cruck to a position above the cruck foot. A wall of wattle, turf, or in later times of stone, was built up to a wall plate carried on the crosspiece ends. From the wall plate spars sloped up to a roof tree or ridge pole carried on the top of the crucks, and thatch was laid upon them for roofing. Such a house was extended simply by adding another bay.

This cruck method of building is restricted to part of the highland zone, including the North York Moors, and because of its absence from East Anglia and other areas of dominant Anglian settlement, it has been regarded as being probably of Norse origin and of being in use only where Norse influence was strong. Nearly all the cruck buildings were replaced by stone structures in the great sixteenth and seventeenth century rebuildings, but in the dales areas a few small examples have survived, generally as farm buildings. A few crucks incorporated in the gable walls of stone rebuilding have been discovered in recent demolition or alteration work, and a few entire buildings and more single crucks have been preserved either *in situ* or in 'folk museums'.[1]

In the north-west part of the Riding, on the limestone ground, where heavy forest trees were few and the tree cover was of lighter trees and scrub, this early timber building was soon replaced in the abundant stone, or was of so slight a structure as not to have survived at all. In the Coal Measure areas, where clay soils are abundant and oak could grow to perfection, crucks of massive timber have survived to the present. Around Halifax, Huddersfield, and Sheffield, crucks were used in large timber buildings which were often extended into timber-framed small halls which have only been replaced or removed in recent years at a time when there was sufficient interest to secure their complete recording and full description.

Cruck houses were being built and are documented from the fourteenth century and even as late as the early seventeenth, but especially in the Calder and Colne valleys another type of structure, the rectangular timber framed house was evolving. This is more akin to the timber and half-timber houses of the Midlands and the plains, a rectangular house with vertical side posts carrying a king-post truss across their tops. Side walls and gables were framed

[1] S. O. Addy, *The Evolution of the English House*, 1910; J. Walton, 'Cruck framed buildings in Yorkshire', *Yorkshire Archaeological Journal*, 37, 1948, pp. 49–66.

with more or less elaborate timber work and infilling and were finished off with wattle and plaster (Plate 10).

In the dales of Craven and the north-west the dissolution of the monasteries set off a series of events which resulted in a great rebuilding of the smaller housing in stone. The property and estates of the monasteries was valued and through the Augmentation Office, the Crown, to which the property had been confiscated, sold many of them as complete estates. This was the opportunity for wealthy merchants, grocers, and traders of London, and those country families who had means to speculate, not with the intention of keeping and developing the estates, but of breaking them up for resale at a profit. Some of the purchasers used the monastic ruins as a quarry from which they built country mansions for themselves, or adapted part of the monastic buildings by reshaping and extending them to the same purpose. We shall discuss some examples of this when we are looking at the larger halls and parks. Many of the farms particularly those on remote granges were mortgaged to the sitting tenants, or sold to some local person as an estate, later to be broken up and disposed of by him during the following fifty years.

In upper Airedale, the manor of Malham East which had been a grange of Bolton Priory, was bought eventually by Lambert[2] and parts of the land and individual farms were then sold by him at various dates. Bordley estates of Bolton had been bought from the purchaser of the Priory by three speculators who in turn sold off the farms and parcels of land to the tenants so creating a township of freeholders. The estates of Fountains Abbey were bought by Sir Richard Gresham, a London merchant, for £10,122 18s. 4d., which was arrived at by taking the annual value as shown in a survey of 1540 and taking twenty times this rent as the price.

[2] John Lambert of Calton in Kirkby Malham parish; great-grandfather of General Lambert of the Civil War.

Soon after the purchase Gresham sold off several townships, Brimham, Winsley, Warsill, Hartwith, Dacre, and Bewerley in Nidderdale, to Sir Arthur Darcy. Darcy held the estates for only twenty years, taking rents as a return on his investment. The township of Bewerley was sold to a Westmorland purchaser, but in Hartwith and Winsley about half of the tenants were allowed to buy their own tenement. The remainder of Hartwith and Winsley was sold to the family of Ingilby of Ripley Castle, along with Dacre, and they in turn recovered their purchase price by selling seven farms to the occupants. It was later, around 1590 that the Greshams sold many farms in the upper dale and then disposed of the remaining estate to Sir Stephen Proctor. By the mid years of the seventeenth century, after one or two generations, these farmers were sufficiently prosperous from wool-rearing and farming to consider replacing their now very old and constricted dwellings with something better and more worthy of their new freehold position. It was thus that the great rebuilding came about, mainly of small farmhouses, although a few who had speculated in property were able to build something larger, small halls and large yeoman houses. In some of the estates in Nidderdale, such as those bought by the Yorke family, farms were not sold but were leased out on leases for 3000 years at an annual rent, with payments to be made at every change of tenant by sale or inheritance.[3] This kind of lease gave the same degree of security as did outright purchase, so the rebuilding took place on these estates as well. This extensive change of ownership of land, breaking up large estates into numerous small freeholds was taking place over most of the Pennine area where the many monastic communities had possessed granges of large extent, mainly sheep farms or remote dale properties. The richer arable lands of the lowlands were generally bought in by wealthy families or

[3] B. Jennings (Ed.), *A History of Nidderdale,* 1967, part Chap. VII.

merchants, and kept by them as estates of squirearchy with the very minimum of sales to the small tenantry. In such areas there is an entirely different pattern of building.

Several writers on Yorkshire and many visitors have time after time commented on the 'traditional' building style displayed by the older cottages and farmhouses. A more intimate knowledge of the county, however, would soon reveal that what is taken for a traditional style is such only for a limited area, and that there are several smaller regions within even the West Riding in which there are characteristics and details which are peculiar to those regions. It might be true to say that over the Pennines there is a basic similarity in the seventeenth and eighteenth century styles of building but that this has very distinctive expressions in different parts, and that these regions are fairly sharply defined. In the north-west, say in the valleys of the Lune and Rawthey, in Dentdale and Garsdale, and the villages eastward towards Ribblesdale, there is a sense of unity, a style in the smaller buildings which one recognises as being common to that area. In Ribblesdale and in the dales east of it, Airedale, Wharfedale and Nidderdale, a comparable style is seen, but any careful look at the buildings shows clearly the absence of some features and substitution of others that will at once 'localise' the buildings. [4]

Right through the 'stone' district of Bradford, Halifax, Huddersfield, and down to Sheffield, the cottages of this period have an appearance which belongs to the district and to no other, although a casual glance will show the familiar long, low building, with mullioned windows, stone-slate roof, and so on, which have already been seen further north and west. There is an overall pattern that belongs to the Pennines which will be absent from the richer arable areas of the vales of York and Trent. Materials and climate account for some of these differences, but

[4] A. Raistrick, *The Pennine Dales*, 1968, Chap. 9, 'Vernacular Architecture'.

occupation, social history, and social structure have also had their influence. In the north-west area, around Sedbergh and the dales coming to the Lune, the settlement was dominantly Norse, and the chief occupation is farming based on sheep-rearing with a supplementary dairy farming or cattle-rearing. Following Norse custom, small farms are scattered and most of the small enclosures of each farm, have their 'laithe', a combined hay barn and, within it, cow-standings, in which a few, four or five, cattle will over-winter, near which they will be milked, and their manure will be spread on the field around the laithe. The hay of that land will be kept in the laithe and fed to those cattle through the winter. Thus there is a very intimate link of a small group of cattle with their own small area of land and its hay crop. The farm thus needs no large buildings near the house. The house is small, a cottage with little more than a few outhouses. The sheep have their folds for gathering, but spend most or all of the year out of doors. The cottages in this area are thus living accommodation only.

The Yoredale Series of rocks which make much of this area provides some good sandstone which breaks easily into thinnish, roughly rectangular blocks, naturally, so the building is comparable, on a rough scale, to building with brick, or squared and sized stone. This sandstone is easily built into squared openings, doors and windows, and these can be made without the need for specially cut jambs and side pieces. Lintels and doorheads can be made from the numerous large flags which occur in the series, and which are quarried mainly for floors. The shape of doorways, and windows, and the plan of the house, one room thick and two or three long, are like those of the rest of the Pennines, but the whole wall space acquires a measure of uniformity with these well coloured, yellow-brown stones approximately matched in size. Occasionally on the better cottages and farms, the windows have been framed with cut stone and have mullions resembling those of other Pennine areas, but these are the exception not the rule. The thinness of the large flags makes them unsuited for spanning a wide opening so that the windows of the Sedbergh district tend to be noticeably smaller than those of most other areas. The roofs are of grey slate, thin flagstone which in this area is abundant and has been quarried for sale over a considerably wider area.

A feature which distinguishes this area from the others is that of the chimneys. They take much of the character of those in the buildings in the adjacent south of Westmorland. Round chimney-stacks are common and these are very often carried on a massive square basal section. This in turn either comes up from ground level as a projection on the gable, or it is carried on massive corbels built out from the gable at about the level of the eaves. These corbelled and round chimneys are a distinctive feature all over the north-west district.

In Craven and the dales where limestone is the main rock, it is used in random or rubble walling and a building thus requires good sandstone or carefully dressed limestone quoins to bind it at the corners, and all openings have to be framed in well-cut sandstone. The quoins, door, and window openings and jambs, lintels and sills are thus the work of the stone-mason as distinct from the waller and they offer scope for some amount of personal distinction in small mouldings, chamfered edges and other personal quirks. Many of the cottages and farmhouses of this re-building carry a date over the door, usually a dominant initial, that of the surname, and two others, one each of man and wife, with the date, all contained in more or less ornate surrounds, varying from the simple rectangle for all or for individual letters, to highly curved and moulded enclosures in Ribblesdale doorways. These dates lie generally within the period 1640 to 1740 with very few earlier or later.

In the stone country south of Airedale good building stones are everywhere common and the builder-mason can use cut stone for all parts. This avoids the rugged appearance of much of the dales building, gives a smooth, well finished look and makes an attractive building without the necessity for minor ornament to set it off. This of course is not entirely absent but is frequently almost limited to ornaments on the gable peaks and corners, and the hood moulding over windows. As soon as the textile zone is entered, however, there appears a unique distinguishing feature, the weaving window. In the cottages of the late seventeenth and early eighteenth centuries the principal occupation became handloom weaving. There was little room in the 'house-place' or living room for a cumbrous loom so that it soon became customary to place this on the first floor against the window. To ensure adequate light the windows were lengthened horizontally and in many cottages one sees the unbalance of two or three light mullioned windows on the ground floor, with a five or six light window above them.⁵ It became the occasional practice, particularly in the eighteenth century, to build two or three cottages in a continuous block and to have a joint 'weaving shop' on the first floor. With this arrangement it is not uncommon to see ten, eleven, twelve or even more light windows on the first floor of the block. Such especially long windows to a weaving shop can also occur in the rather more substantial house of a small clothier who could keep two or three apprentices and perhaps a journeyman at work while he took and fetched from market and cloth hall (Plate 11).

A natural development of this weaving shop practice was the building of 'folds'. These were co-operative efforts, where a piece of land, usually away from the immediate village, was bought and a square of houses built looking

⁵ W. B. Crump and G. Ghorbal, *History of the Huddersfield Woollen Industry*, Tolson Museum Handbook, IX, 1935. Many useful illustrations.

inwards into the fold. The upper floor of the fold was often continuous over all the houses, and in this huge attic would be established the combing and preparing of raw wool, spinning and weaving, trades to occupy most of the men and many of the women and girls of the fold. One such square has only recently disappeared from Skipton, on the outskirts of the town as it then was, Union Square. The attic was continuous in this way, and combing, spinning and weaving were all carried on co-operatively, the many families in fact acting as a small manufacturing company, with one leading man to act as manager and salesman. This group was active until finally displaced by power looms established in the mills of the town, but had been working well for two or three generations.

There is a change in the appearance of the labourers' cottages and farm buildings as soon as one moves off the Pennine slopes. The most noticeable change of course is in the building materials, but another factor which contributes to the difference is the social structure of the lowland area of arable farming. In this lower ground, the manorial structure of the community has persisted until recent times, and there are many large estates which may include the whole, or nearly the whole, of a village. In the population of such villages there is a far smaller proportion of freeholders owning their own house or having anything corresponding to a small-holding farm. There is a stronger differentiation between the farms which are generally large and the very small cottages of the labouring population.

In the seventeenth century, when the rebuilding of the Pennine houses in stone was taking place, rebuilding on the lowlands was not yet very much advanced. On the whole it began later, towards the end of that century, or even well on into the eighteenth. There was a wide use of brick in the parishes east of the Magnesian Limestone belt, and in most villages the bricks were made on the spot as required. The cover of glacial deposits usually provided for at least some patches of suitable brick clay, and two men working together could make about 80,000 bricks in a year. There were itinerant companies of brick-maker families, who could settle for a whole season if the demand were there. The brick cottages were often small compared with the Pennine cottages and in the Trent and lower Ouse valleys two-roomed one-storey houses were the commonest type with thatch still in general use for roofing. With the growth of continental trade into Hull and York, however, pantiles were introduced from Holland, and soon became the commonest roofing material. The general picture then in these lower valley areas was one of nucleated villages with red or brown brick buildings with red pantile roofs. Among the larger cottages and small farms there are some examples of a mixed timber and brick structure, or on the Magnesian Limestone area and even in the Pennines around Halifax and Huddersfield, of timber and stone building. In a two-storied building the lower storey is built in stone or brick but the rest of the house is in timber-framing, with wattle filling and clay daubed or plastered in the better buildings. Such mixed style buildings were mainly of the later seventeenth and early eighteenth century. On the Pennines they were made robust enough to carry a stone-slate roof, but on the lowland they used either thatch or pantiles.

Among the rebuilding a feature over the whole of the county was the enlargement of the farmhouses.[6] In the Pennines the basic plan was long, usually a kitchen-living room and a parlour with a loft over both, with accommodation for hay and stock in a continuation of the building under the single roof. The rebuilding in stone gave a long, low mass, the windows now larger and divided by stone mullions and usually the plan included an additional room

[6] M. W. Barley, *The English Farmhouse and Cottage*, 1961.

added at the end away from the barn. Party walls between the rooms replaced the crucks and were taken up to support the heavy stone roof which was otherwise carried on heavy king-post trusses. Doorways in these party walls on what was now the permanent bedroom flooring level gave three bedrooms, opening one from the other, and corresponding to the ground floor rooms. A stone stairway was often built from an offshut at the back which accommodated an added back kitchen.

On the Pennines from Airedale to the south a frequent type of larger farmer-clothier house was the small hall of common mediaeval H-plan. A central hall going up to the roof is flanked by a cross wing at each end, one end the service area and the other end the domestic family rooms. Some of these halls were timber-framed but in the stone districts many were built of stone from the fifteenth and early sixteenth centuries. Many timber examples were, in the seventeenth century, cased or extended in stone like the fine example at Shibden Hall, Halifax. These 'halls' are sufficiently numerous to be a prominent feature all through the textile area and they range in size from the 'small halls' of the clothiers to be found in many of the villages to the large ones like Bolling Hall, Bradford, and even larger, with additions and elaborations in great variety. A modest copying of this form is seen in many houses where a large central living room with a long, mullioned window, sometimes of extra height, has on each side of it other rooms above which the front wall is carried up into gables which simulate the ends of the cross wings. This frontage with gables is found over all the Pennines except the north-west, and can be regarded, from its frequency, almost as a traditional style.

The larger farms in the lower Ouse and Trent valleys were in the main, of eighteenth century rebuilding. A square plan of Georgian inspiration replaced the long house plan. The house was generally detached from the farm buildings and developed its plan and surroundings independent of them. There are more such groups of farmhouses and farm buildings, including perhaps one or two agricultural labourers' cottages, away from the village nucleus and on the fringe of former open field between them and the in-taken and newly enclosed pasture or waste. In these areas the village field pattern extends almost to the boundary of the next manor or township and the effect is one of a continuous countryside of fields and farms with a regular sprinkling of villages, each with its church and manor as the focal point in the architecture.

The textile inventions and the spread of the coke-smelting for iron, with the increase in steel production, forming together the basis of the Industrial Revolution, were the reasons for a new style of building in and around the industrial centres. The factory system so essential a part of the textile revolution brought large numbers of workers from the rural areas into the growing towns and forced upon both employers and the parish authorities demands for housing on a scale not previously experienced. The agricultural areas missed all the comparable pressures and, except for the improvement of cottages, many villages were able to continue their eighteenth century picture right through the nineteenth, and often into the twentieth century.

For the bulk of the industrial housing we must look to the towns and the overgrown villages on the fringes of the industrial areas. The basic change which alters the whole scene in a drastic manner and which completely changes the house plan, appearance, and architectural detail, as compared with all we have so far discussed, is the introduction of terraced housing of uniform pattern. The repetition of a single type of dwelling in continuous rows of a score or two of absolutely identical houses, and such rows repeated time after time, in some of the larger industrial towns, to form whole districts, is something without any previous parallel. In the earlier housing, even that of the labouring peasant we have been looking at types capable of infinite small variation, small quirks of personal fancy of the builder, differing response to the character of the material and the situation. Windows and chimneys related in size and position to the internal plan and the functions of rooms, a pattern and texture of walling responding to the variations of irregular-sized rubble or random stone, to the variation of hand-made brick with the custom of the maker and the local variations of the clay and the burning.

All this is lost in the new building. A plan acceptable to the builder is slavishly followed: materials, size of cut stone, of bricks, of windows and of all details are settled once for all. The original adaptation of a plan which will allow the most profitable repetition now determine the form of the working-class home. Mass production of environment has arrived with the degradation of men, women and children to the status of so many 'hands' to be counted in identical terms with so many 'spindles', 'looms' or 'frames' which together make up the 'mill'.

It hardly seems possible to include this affront to human dignity under the decent label of 'vernacular architecture', but for the sake of completeness we cannot dismiss this, the major part of the nineteenth century building in the industrial towns. In contemplating much of this building it is very difficult to smother anger and disgust. Although much of the worst of this housing is now being demolished, enough still remains to form an important part of the visual scene. We can be thankful that the conditions of this housing and the factory life which it reflects bred a small core of rebels from whom came, in spite of poverty and persecution, the Trade Unions, the Co-operative movement, the redeeming fellowship of the non-conformist chapels and, eventually, the reforming pressures within the local government authorities which are now sweeping away this hideous section of our larger cities.

The basic plans of this housing follow two principal patterns, the two- and the four-roomed house. Many of the two-roomed houses were of the much abused (though the abuse is not always merited) 'back-to-back' type. A rather broad (or should it be deep?) row of houses is seen as a long succession of doorway, window, window, doorway, passage, doorway, window, window, doorway, passage, and this succession repeated for the length of the row. Go through the passage, which is only a ground floor feature, and you enter a yard with the balanced doorway, window, each side of the passage opening. At the bottom of the very small yard, there are two earth closets (most of these now converted to water closet) shared by four households. Each house is alike—the door opens directly into the living room-kitchen from which rises, behind a door in one corner, a steep stair to a tiny room over the passage and bedroom over the kitchen-living room. There may, according to the situation, be another door from the kitchen, leading into a useful place, the 'cellar-head', containing a sink with cold water and the steps to a small cellar. Failing this, the sink is in a cupboard in the corner between fireplace and window. All are exactly alike except for the alternating left- and right-hand arrangement each side of the passage, and the alternate house with the advantage of the little room over the passage.

The non-back-to-back house is one room wide along the street. The door again opens into the front room, in the better type cut off in a narrow passage which leads to the bottom of a staircase between the two rooms. The back room is larger, a kitchen-living room, which in later types may have a narrow extension of scullery taking one side of a narrow paved yard, with the closet opening from the yard at the remote end. Upstairs there are two bedrooms and in some 'better' houses, a small room over the scullery extension. The face of all these rows is moulded to one single pattern of regularly repeated doorway and window arrangement, with no relief from end to end of the apparently interminable street. The front street is wide enough for a delivery cart, the back street is often a narrow alley the very minimum width for access to the back. In the back-to-back there is no back street, yard backs on to yard and the back house windows glare at short range at their opposing 'neighbour' across the closets and ashpits. In Leeds, however, the back-to-back houses differ in the rows being separated by a wide street between *every* set of back-to-backs, and so avoiding any passages into a totally enclosed back yard.

A feature of slightly later dating, at the end of the nineteenth and in the early twentieth centuries, is the appearance of a narrow strip of 'garden' at the front, often no more than six feet, the use of a bay window at ground floor level and a slight featuring of the door. The rooms are a little larger and thousands of housewives looked forward to being promoted to one of these 'better class' streets. The more venturous of these streets supplied a bath, sometimes in the scullery, sometimes, height of ambition, upstairs. Many rows of these houses are of sound structure, capable of modernisation into acceptable dwellings which can still serve another generation.

To turn away from the smaller buildings which house the majority of our population, we must look, at least briefly, to the larger mansions and country houses which, in spite of all the misconceptions of the West Riding as a continuum of industrial landscapes, are numerous, of architectural merit, and contribute many thousands of acres of fine landscaped parkland. There are in the county a small number of sixteenth century houses which originated at the dissolution of the monasteries. Some of the purchasers of monastic estates, after the sale of land to recover the purchase price, turned to the provision of a mansion for themselves. In a few cases this consisted only of an improvement or extension of a monastic building, as at Bolton Priory. The estates of the priory were purchased by the first Earl of Cumberland, who retained the great gatehouse for a house for himself or his bailiff. In the eighteenth century much stone from the priory was used to make extensions at each side of the gatehouse and so produce the present Bolton Hall, with much of the demesne and surrounds of the Priory and its woods as its park.[7]

At Nostel Priory and Roche Abbey new mansions were built of stone taken from the monastic buildings and great parks were created by the arts of the eighteenth century landscape gardeners. One of the most impressive of these estates is at Fountains Abbey, near Ripon. This abbey and its properties was sold to Sir Richard Gresham, a wealthy London merchant. He soon sold off much of the outlying estates, granges, farms, and manors, but for a time retained the abbey and its grounds. These and the remainder of the estates were sold in 1597 to Sir Stephen Proctor who between 1603 and 1607 built a splendid house in Elizabethan style, Fountains Hall, not far from the abbey ruins. The extensive grounds of the abbey were kept as a park for the Hall, but in 1627 the park and hall passed into the possession of Richard Evans and by the marriage of his daughter to John Messenger of Newsham into that family. In 1767 the Hall, the abbey and its grounds were sold to William Aislebie of Studley. The Aislebies had been at Studley from 1674, and in 1720 began to plan and develop the park which was eventually extended to 650 acres. After

---

[7] Brief descriptions of most of the larger houses will be found in N. Pevsner, *The Buildings of England. Yorkshire West Riding*, 1967.

1767 William Aislebie and his son John began planning the Studley Park and the Fountains Abbey grounds as a single designed park which was later regarded as one of the triumphs of landscape gardening. The deep valley of the river Skell in which the abbey nestles was converted into half garden, half park, with ornamental ponds, small falls and other water features constructed by controlling the Skell. Small temples, belvederes and pavilions, with a magnificent 'surprize view' of the abbey make this one of the finest of all designed landscapes in the north.

Nostel Priory, five miles east of Wakefield and four miles south of Pontefract, was, like Bolton, an Augustinian priory. It was given by Henry VIII, in 1540, to Dr Thomas Leigh, visitor of the monasteries, and eventually by a series of sales passed into the possession of George Winn and was inherited by Sir Rowland Winn. In 1733 a magnificent Georgian mansion was built to the designs of James Paine and a wing was added in 1766 by Robert Adam. Adam also designed most of the state rooms and Chippendale designed the furniture for them. The great park is crossed by the Wakefield to Doncaster main road, which is carried across the great lake.

The Earl of Scarbrough created a park and erected a fine mansion from the grounds and stone of Roche Abbey near Rotherham. The abbey grounds and the much later abbey house at Kirkstall now form one of Leeds city's excellent parks and museums. It is only excelled by another Leeds museum, Temple Newsam, a former house of the Knights Templar. The oldest part of the great mansion was built in 1544 and additions were made in 1622 by Sir Arthur Ingram and further additions date in later periods. It has been called the Hampton Court of the North, and the house and its park of 935 acres certainly deserve this title (Plate 12).

There are many smaller monastic estates which provided

the material for small country houses, with or without parks. Kirklees Priory, a Cistercian nunnery near Wakefield, was kept as Kirklees Park and the conventional buildings were used for a house, later rebuilt not far away as a mansion. Monk Bretton Priory near Barnsley is only to be recognised by fragments and foundations among farm buildings. In the earlier history of the county there have been two series of parks which contributed to the landscape, the parks and chases of mediaeval times, most of which are now gone, and the group of parks initiated as the precincts of monastic houses. These latter have generally been absorbed into parks of the eighteenth century, to which period most parks in the county belong.

The eighteenth century saw great fortunes being made by landowners benefiting from the exploitation of coal and other minerals in their land, brought into great demand and value by the progress of the Industrial Revolution. The Duke of Norfolk contributed through his mineral wealth and its exploitation to the expansion of Sheffield. The appreciation of land values and the rapidly increasing demand for agricultural products brought to many of the landowners incomes of several thousand pounds a year. The great landowners near expanding towns sold land profitably for the new housing and industrial sites and this action has been repeated in the twentieth century as the new collieries were sunk and new towns were built in the midst of the belt of park lands. Sufficient of the parks remain, however, to form a very significant part of the landscape and to be worthy of some comment, although this is not the place for any detailed history or treatment. Greenwood's map of the West Riding, 1817, shows seventy-six parks with a total area of some 23,000 acres. There was considerable variation in size but three at least, Harewood, Bramham, and Wentworth Woodhouse, were each over 1000 acres, while seven more were between 500 and 1000 acres. Such areas of parkland as these constitute major features in their local landscape and in most cases they have suffered little subsequent change, so that we can with a degree of truth say that in them we are looking at a well preserved eighteenth century countryside.

Capability Brown had in the eighteenth century made an art of designing a park landscape with plantations, water and vistas, with little appearance of artificiality. Many of Brown's parks were 'improved' by Repton though he adhered closely to Brown's general principle of using the natural shape of the ground, with the planting of trees and control of water features to enhance it. Both Brown and Repton were responsible between 1760 and 1820 for the creation of many parks in the West Riding which have not been materially altered since that time.[8]

A study of the map will show that there is an almost continuous sequence of parks stretching from north to south along the belt of the Magnesian Limestone from Sleningford at the northern border near Tanfield, down to Sandbeck at Roche Abbey near the southern boundary (Fig. 10). Most of the larger parks, however, are on the wooded ground of the Middle Coal Measures except Harewood which is on Millstone Grit. Between Wakefield and Barnsley a belt of parks lies across the Coal Measure soils from Nostel Priory, by Chevet, Woolley, Bretton, and Cannon Hall, with some smaller ones. Some of the larger parks and halls of this group now occupy an important place in the life of the community. Bretton and Woolley Halls and parks were bought by the County Council and Wentworth Castle near Barnsley by Barnsley Corporation. Bretton is now a Teachers' Training College specialising

[8] An excellent study of some of the West Riding parks has been made by Bryan E. Coates, 'Park Landscapes of the E. & W. Ridings in the time of Humphry Repton', *Yorkshire Archaeological Journal*, XLI, 1965. Also thesis presented at Leeds University, September 1960.

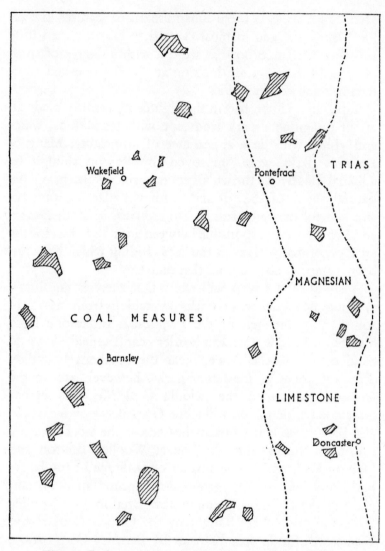

Fig. 10. Park areas in part of the industrial West Riding.

in music and drama: Woolley Hall is a college at which courses are given for teachers from the whole of the West Riding schools, revision courses and long weekend or longer courses on special subjects. This gracious hall has won a very warm place in the affections of the teachers and is contributing materially to the quality of teaching within the county. Wentworth Castle (a magnificent hall, castle only in name) is a Training College of the Barnsley County Borough authority and Wentworth Woodhouse, nearer Sheffield, said to be the largest mansion in England, is leased by the West Riding authority as a Training College for teachers in physical education. Cannon Hall is a museum set in a splendid park and serves the Barnsley and surrounding area as Temple Newsam serves Leeds. Fountains Hall and Abbey are similarly open to the public and much of the Studley Royal Park, both purchased by the West Riding County Council, is planned to become a 'Country Park' under the provisions of the Countryside Bill, 1968.

Harewood, Bramham, and Nostel are open to the public on certain days and in these various ways many of the largest parks have now been changed from the preserves of the rich landowning families to places for public recreation and for education, and so have become a part of the new landscape to which the public are accustoming themselves. These new uses can never compensate for the appalling exploitation and misery of the workers by which the fortunes which created the parks were acquired, but it is a great encouragement to all who are looking for the social betterment of the nation, that at last these palaces of wealth and ostentation have been brought into public use and service.

If we can return for a moment to the more vernacular architecture of the small house, the prosperity of the farmers in the eighteenth century was reflected in most parts of the county by improvements to his house. Many small farms received a 'new-fashioned' Georgian front, often leaving seventeenth century mullioned windows and other features at the back unchanged. A number of choice Georgian houses were built to replace older property and several were also built on new sites within or near the villages. In many of the agricultural villages these small eighteenth and early nineteenth century gems stand among their seventeenth century companions without any incongruity. The greater part of the Georgian building, however, was located in the smaller market towns outside the industrial areas. There are some larger houses, such as Newby Hall between Boroughbridge and Ripon, redesigned by Adam between 1765 and 1783, which include in the park a display of well-designed gardens in which flowering plants play a very great part. The gardens indeed are often almost as famous as the contents of the house.

BIBLIOGRAPHY

Addy, S. O. *The Evolution of the English House,* 1910.
Barley, M. W. *The English Farm House and Cottage,* London, 1961.
Campbell, M. *The English Yeoman,* 1942.
Pevsner, N. *The Buildings of England. Yorkshire West Riding,* Penguin, 1967.

5. Landscape of the Industrial Revolution: I

Textile cottage industry. Mining. Steel areas. Agriculture.

THE MOST RADICAL changes in the appearance of the West Riding were brought about by the Industrial Revolution, particularly in the century between 1750 and 1850. In some areas the transformation from rural countryside to industrial town was complete. The least change was to be seen in the agricultural areas, though even here the open country was diminished by the enclosure of commons, waste, and the remnants of open field agriculture. The two areas in which the greatest changes were made were those of textiles and the iron industries, followed in less spectacular fashion by the mining industries and transport. It was in this change that landscapes emerged to which one could put a definitive label—one could now begin to speak of a textile landscape, of the iron and steel zone, of an enclosure landscape and so on and point to valid differences. Towns grew into cities in the years following this period, but their main lines were laid down in the changes demanded by growing industry and the new transport.

The agricultural landscape in the middle of the eighteenth century was one of partial open fields around the villages, but enclosure by agreement had already produced large areas of fenced fields. The new fields of these enclosures as we have already discussed in Chapter 3 often reflected the shape of the mediaeval rig and furrow ploughing pattern, the fields being mostly long and narrow and slightly curved. The common pastures and waste were still unenclosed. Great advances in some methods of husbandry such as the work of Tull and Townsend on crop growing and the results of better breeding in sheep and cattle as demonstrated by Bakewell, were changing ideas and methods in all departments of agriculture. With the increasing demand for beef, milk, grain, butter, cheese, and pork arising in the growing industrial populations, what remained of the open fields was doomed to rapid and complete enclosure. In the western districts of the dales the arable fields were already turned to pasture and meadow for stock-rearing and dairying. The change brought about by the new wave of enclosure was the creation of rectangular fields, small, roughly square fields of about ten or twelve acres or even less, these being more economical for stock-rearing than were much larger fields. Many of the long fields previously enclosed were now divided by cross-walls, and an approximate checker-board pattern was produced, set out by hedges except in the west where stone walls dominated the scene.

In the lowland townships on richer soils the common pastures were enclosed and turned to arable and the waste was attacked, to be improved by enclosure to replace the lost pasture. Down the vale of York and Trent the country approached more and more towards a uniform landscape of regular fields, villages evenly spaced among them and parish boundaries only marked by an occasional strip of common or by woodland and plantation kept more for its value to the game preserver and huntsman than as a part of the village economy.

When the surveyors for the Board of Agriculture visited the West Riding in 1794 they kept a journal which brings into highlight the changes of agriculture seen as they moved through the different parts.[1] In the lowland plain

[1] Rennie, Broun, and Shirreff, *General View of the Agriculture of the West Riding of Yorkshire,* 1794, pp. 102–40.

there were still the remnants of common fields, not in very good condition, but oats, wheat, and barley were normal crops, with some turnips. Few commons are mentioned except around Doncaster and the eastern edge towards Hatfield and Thorne. Going towards the Pennines, the chief interest becomes the markets at Ripon and Knaresborough, with their trade in cattle and some sheep, and in dairy produce. Nidderdale is reported as being entirely enclosed with small stone-walled fields and the farms, small in size, as producing butter for the market at York, eventually to be sent to London, and oatmeal-fed hogs, the hams for London and the fat carcases for the industrial towns of Lancashire. Little but dairy cattle is bred, and most of the farmers combine another trade with their farming. Here we are passing into the regular western pattern where mining, quarrying, and textiles are combined with smallholder farming. In Nidderdale the flax industry and the lead-mining were the second occupations, and with these to help, the small farms spread up the hillsides to about 1000 feet above sea level.

In upper Wharfedale and about Skipton and Settle there was much feeding of dairy cattle on the lower ground and the feeding of Scotch cattle and sheep on the uplands, with strong markets at Skipton and Settle, into both of which corn was brought from Knaresborough and Richmond, so that all the land was laid down to pasture and meadow. In the extreme north-west in Dentdale, there was a complete enclosure of the valley land in very small fields, and dairy farming provided great quantities of butter and cheese for Skipton market. The upland pastures were reserved almost entirely for sheep-rearing. In the more southerly farming area the sheep were drawn from Penistone market on the higher Pennines, which is clearly seen as the central market for a wide sheep-rearing area. The intermediate coalfield ground is largely mixed farming, some dairying, some sheep, and a little arable. The trend to farmer-industrial worker seen in Nidderdale is carried to its completion in the textile areas of the Calder and Colne valleys.

The monastic granges had set the pattern of wool production, and had built up the flocks of sheep and done something to improve the breed.[2] At the dissolution the purchasers of the monastic estates had little option but to allow tenants of the abbeys to acquire their tenements by purchase or mortgage, and with them take over the sheep running thereon. Wool now grown by large numbers of small producers was gathered in by the 'wool drivers' who became the middlemen between the farmer and the merchants or clothiers. Away from the monastic estates the wool had either been bought in by the drivers and carried to the markets or had been spun and woven into cloth locally. This trade had given rise before the fourteenth century to the fulling mills, necessary for the finishing of cloth, and by 1400 fulling mills had been built on many of the Yorkshire streams. It was possible in a small mill to combine fulling with corn-milling and there were several corn and fulling mills along the rivers Aire, Calder, and Colne, and soon others were being built solely for fulling. The clothing industry could be encouraged and helped by building fulling mills where independent weavers could bring their cloth to be fulled at a regular charge.

Acts of Parliament in the sixteenth century had established the wool staplers as the only people allowed to deal in raw wool, but the resistance of the West Riding people secured the modification in the Halifax Act of 1555 by which the wool driver was authorised to continue his travels through the dales, purchasing wool in small parcels and bringing it into Halifax market, there to sell it to the recognised clothiers. The clothiers cleaned, oiled, and carded it, or had this done by cottagers, then sent it out by

[2] D. Knowles, *The Religious Orders in England*, 1950, pp. 64–74.

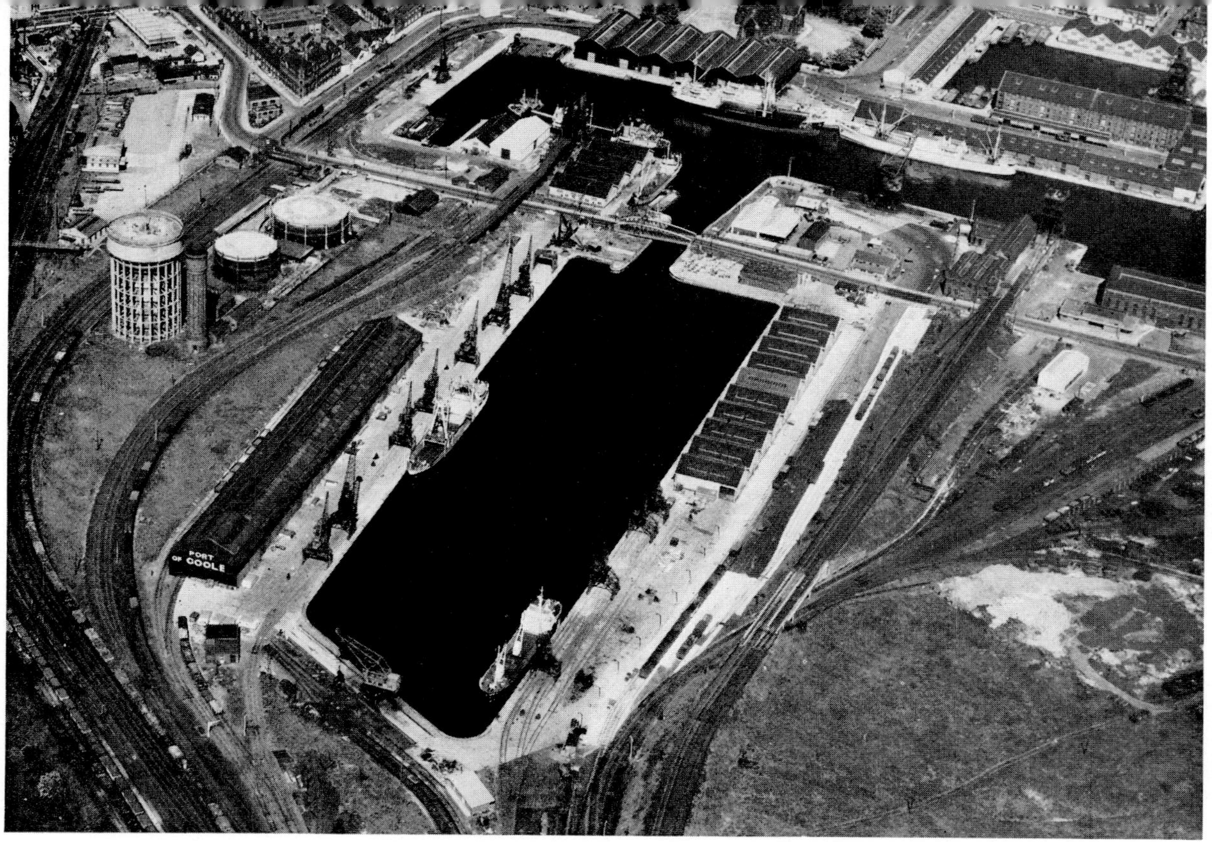

Plate 17 Goole. West Dock, Stanhope Dock and part of Railway Dock.

C. H. Wood

Bertram

Plate 18 Coal barge entering the Sheffield and South Yorkshire Navigation at Sprotborough Lock. Opening from the river Don not far below Doncaster.

Plate 19 Five Rise Locks, Bingley, on the Leeds and Liverpool Canal. The mills are aligned on the canal bank.

G. D. Bolton

G. D. Bolton

Plate 20 Hebden Bridge. Mills are on canal and river; typical industrial terrace housing on the hillside. Heptonstall is on the hill top. On a steep hill like this, the four-storey houses are often double; two floors make a bottom house and two upper floors, entered from the hillside behind, make a 'top' house. Other complete four-storey houses were built as lodging houses for the textile workers.

the drivers into the homesteads over a wide countryside. The spun yarn was again collected and carried back to the small towns or put out to cottagers for weaving. The preamble to the Act of 1555 says of the drivers that wool is to be "brought by them to the Towne of Halifaxe, and there to sell the same to suche poore folkes of that and other parishes adjoyning as shall work the same in Cloth or yarn". It speaks of the local men, small 'clothiers' who went to Halifax market "ther to bye upon the woolldryver some a stone, some two and some three or four accordinge to theyre habilitee, and to carry the same to their houses, some 3, 4, 5 and 6 myles of, upon their Headdes and Backes" to convert it there either into yarn or cloth.

As these heavy burdens were to be carried to and from market, and equal burdens of cloth to and from the fulling mill and the finishers' premises, the weavers, when they could accomplish it, settled near the markets and contrived if they were not too poor, to keep a horse or pony. It was the pressure of this poverty and labour which led to the widespread 'intake' on the waste land and moor edges, on the land above the township fields and pastures and well above the settled valley farms. A smallholding of even half to one acre could be made to provide some food, milk, cheese, and eggs with the help of pasture on the waste and commons. Feeding for a goose or a cow and pasture for a pony could be contrived by a careful man. The men were the weavers and the women and girls spun and generally looked after the house and the livestock. The structure of this industry involved a great deal of transport of material—the wool driver brought in wool from a very wide area to the market; it was carried out to be spun and in many cases the yarn went back to the market to be carried again to the weaver; cloth went to the fuller and the finisher and again back to market. Pack-horse roads converging on the markets, mill roads leading to and from the fulling mills on the main rivers; cottages and smallholdings along the valley crest fringing the moors where the cottages were half farm, half textile workshop, these were the elements of a new landscape which soon dominated the Calder and Colne valleys in the eighteenth century.

As the domestic industry increased it became possible for groups of spinners and weavers to come closer together, to work continuously in wool and to make a living, poor though it might be, without the farming adjunct, getting food in the markets to which they took their cloth. So, around these valleys and on the high ground between Huddersfield, Halifax, and Bradford we find a high-level zone of cottages overlooking the valleys from the moor edge, built of the local excellent building stone and so avoiding the appearance of poverty. Many of them have the 'weaving windows' discussed in Chapter 4. From place to place there are the small aggregates of cottages in 'folds' or in tiny hamlets of weavers, where later the warehouse and small factory of the embryo manufacturer was located, to become still later the centre of one of the many small mill villages.[3]

Some of the old established villages continued with farms as their primary feature and with cottage textiles occupying a proportion of their population, but in these villages the two occupations tended to be kept apart and the buildings are clearly different, the textile cottages being frequently an obvious infilling of a more open and older village grouping. These older villages are fairly numerous and with the migration of the greater part of industry into the valleys, they have managed to retain much of their seventeenth and eighteenth century appearance and architecture. Heptonstall, Sowerby, Rastrick, Soyland, Norland, Lindley, Slaithwaite, and a dozen others were such villages, with a core of seventeenth century houses in which

[3] Crump and Ghorbal, *op. cit.*

most are small cottage properties but some are farmsteads.

Standing on the edge of the moors almost anywhere along these valleys, the Calder, Colne or their main tributaries, one can look out across a unique landscape, often of great though not conventional beauty. The scene is an epitome of long years and even of centuries of social and economic evolution and one can strip away century after century of accretion until the naked Pennine scene of magnificent high plateau and deep-cut valleys and ravines is all that remains.

The moors covered either with heather or with benty grass, still carry their flocks of sheep and the likeliest person to meet is the shepherd with his dog. There may be the tip-heaps of a quarry and the skeleton figure of the quarry crane near at hand, or at least within sight on the moor, and the same skeleton figures may often be seen across the valley and showing up on the ridges between the main valley and its tributaries. Boyhood memories of these great moorlands seem now, in recollection, to be compounded of heather, sheep, grouse, and the excitement of quarries, a few of them still working and all to be explored (Plate 13). Little else remains, but to the end of life I shall find it difficult to pass a quarry without an exploration of its old dressing sheds and a knowing look at the 'lifts' of rock, their qualities learned and absorbed from old quarrymen in early years and now ineradicable.

Towards the valley the broad shelf below the moor is cut up in small fields, many of the walls now broken and neglected as the intakes go back to the wild, the quiet greybrown houses scattered at intervals among them often showing a mullioned window or a well-framed doorway that speaks of eighteenth century workmanship. A few of these houses are still occupied but many are forgotten and ruined. Where the fields are greener and the walls better kept there is surely a village, perched up here at the head of a fearful descent to the valley. Few visitors from other parts like these roads with bends and gradients of a miniature alpine character. Today, however, buses with a full load make their way up and down without worry, taking them for granted as a natural feature of the area. These desperately steep banks are in large part clothed in woods and some of the side valleys are beauty spots, widely known and dearly loved by many people (Plate 14). The Hebden valley, Hardcastle Crags, Crimsworth Dene, Ramsden Clough, Luddenden Dean and many others such as the Rivelin valley in Sheffield have a surprising beauty in the midst of widespread industry, the only intrusion being the occasional ruins of an early water-mill. The early fulling mills were many of them situated in these side valleys at a point where there was a ford across the swift stream, where a pack-horse road came zigzagging down the valley side, and where a small dam could impound water for the wheel (Plate 15). Some of these early fords were soon spanned by a delightful, high-arched, single span, 'packhorse' bridge, a few of which remain to be admired by the visitors.

The wooded main valley sides often give a touch of unreality to the crowded mills and industrial housing of the narrow valley bottom against which they seem to impinge. From our viewpoint we look over the forest of mill chimneys which replaces the valley bottom trees. As more and more electric power is used and smokeless zones affect the towns, broad views and long prospects become the normal experience. The plateau of the Pennines stretches for miles, the deep-cut valleys appearing, except for those immediately before us, only as deep scorings, one after another, across this great expanse of moor and upland. The heavy grits which attract the quarries form innumerable 'edges' and 'crags' which define the valleys with the greatest precision. The scene is on such a scale that it would appear that industry had crept quietly into the valleys to hide away the minimum disturbance of the wild moorland tops. It is only in the great Leeds–Bradford–Halifax–Huddersfield conurbation that the nineteenth century has provided a foil to this landscape of the upper valleys by bringing out its industrial building on to the open of the high ground, but even there, small hill farms, fields of rhubarb and occasional 'denes' are not altogether absent, and the rural scene is by no means totally banished.

In the eighteenth century the approach to most of the hamlets and to many of the weavers' cottages would have been given an appearance very strange to one not used to or familiar with the making of cloth. When the cloth was scoured and fulled it was liable to considerable shrinkage as it dried. To prevent or to minimise this 'tenters' were used, and a tenter ground—there are such names as Tenter Croft still to be found in most parts of the textile areas—was the normal adjunct of the house or hamlet. Rows of posts firmly set in the ground, parallel and about the width of a piece of cloth apart had horizontal bars set along their tops. These bars were set with sharp 'tenter hooks' on to which the edges of the cloth were set. As the cloth dried in the open air tenters it was prevented from shrinking. A first edition of the six inches to one mile Ordnance Survey map of almost any part of the textile area shows great numbers of tenters. A century earlier Defoe had been impressed as he approached Halifax and says:

". . . we could see that at almost every house there was a tenter, and almost on every tenter a piece of cloth, or kersie, or shalloon, for they are the three articles of that country's labour; from which the sun glancing and, as I may say, shining (the white reflecting its rays) to us, I thought it was the most agreeable sight that I ever saw . . . yet look which way we would, high to the tops, and low to the bottoms, it was all the same; innumerable houses and tenters, and a white piece upon every tenter... as every clothier must keep a horse, perhaps two to fetch and carry for the use of his manufacture, to fetch home his wool and his provisions from the market, to carry his yarn to the spinners, his manufacture to the fulling mill, and ... to the market to be sold, and the like; so ... [he] keeps a cow or two or more, for his family, and this employs the two or three, or four pieces of enclosed land about his house, for they sow scarce corn enough for their cocks and hens." [4]

In the economy of the West Riding the mining and extractive industries have held an important position for several centuries. There are areas where the many operations of these varied occupations which have had a strong influence and have been responsible for features peculiar to themselves, are still a part of the general scene. Deposits of lead and iron ores, building and road stones, clays for bricks and refractories, and, in the twentieth century, gravel and sand for concrete aggregates, have been extensively worked. The location of these resources is of course dependent upon the geology and varies considerably over much of the county. The lead ores are almost confined to one major field, a tract of a few miles wide running from near Pateley Bridge in Nidderdale, about eighteen miles to near Buckden in upper Wharfedale. On the fringes of this area there are a few small outlying deposits which have had an intermittent mining life of a few score years but have never been more than small producers, with the exception of the Cononley area south of Skipton, which, in spite of less than a century of working, was for a time a very productive area.

It is the fate of almost all extractive industries that their

[4] D. Defoe, *A Tour through England and Wales, 1724–26* (Everyman Edition), 1927, II, p. 194.

early workings are removed in later work or buried under
later spoil so that only the remains of the nineteenth and
occasionally of the eighteenth century work are still visible
except in very few places. This is particularly true of lead-
mining where nearly the whole of the mining scene belongs
to the nineteenth century, the maximum period of development being about 1790 to 1860. Grassington Moor is a
high moorland, 1000 feet to 1200 feet above sea level, on
the north side of Wharfedale and over two miles away from
the river. Over a breadth of about a mile and stretching
along the valley direction beyond the east and west boundaries of the township, it is now a waste of mine spoil heaps
(Plate 16). A careful look at the spoil heaps will soon show
that they lie in straight lines, mostly in an east to west
direction with only a few on cross lines at an angle to the
others. As might be expected the shafts and mine hillocks
follow the veins and as the early mining laws of this area
allocated a regular width of ground on each side of a vein
on which the miner could pile the spoil, this now forms a
narrow belt along the run of each vein. Washing floors,
where ore was crushed and dressed before smelting, fed by
a complex of water courses and with their broad spread of
fine dressing debris, are set among the mines. On the higher
ground reservoirs were made, all but one now empty of
water. At one place on the edge of the Moor the ruins of a
smelt mill with the long flues running up the moor to the
massive chimney are an impressive feature. Roads across
the mines and down to the Turnpike road in the valley complete the picture. Most of what is seen belongs to the period⁵
between 1790 and 1880, by which time the mines ceased to
work.

Greenhow Hill is exceptional in the number of small
houses that are to be seen among the mines, widely scattered
with their small crofts, and many approached by a deeply

⁵ A. Raistrick, *Old Yorkshire Dales*, 1967, Chap. 7.

sunk and very narrow lane. These houses were mostly built following a decision in a Chancery suit of 1613 that

> "there may be cottages erected for the miners and mineral workmen upon the said waste [Greenhow Hill], and some competant quantity of ground to be improved of the said waste and laid to them, and also for the keeping of draught oxen and horses for the maintainance of the mines, always leaving the tenants sufficient common."[6]

Most of the cottages became derelict when the mines closed but in recent years many of them have been renovated for weekend cottages and are bringing a bit of life back to the area. There is a marked difference in the topography of Greenhow Hill and Grassington Moor. Three deep valleys penetrate the Greenhow field so that much of the mining ground was reached by long 'adits', tunnels driven from the stream sides into the hill, which by long working concentrated some of the largest spoil heaps at their mouth. The shafts from the surface of the Hill are more for access and ventilation and though most were used in part for the haulage of ore, their mine hillocks are small compared with those on Grassington Moor where the mines were worked entirely from shafts and where each shaft has a large heap and is a prominent feature in the landscape. The smelt mills on Greenhow are all situated near the adit mouths down in the valleys.

In contrast with the clearly localised occurrence of lead ores, the ores of iron are of common distribution in the Millstone Grit and the Coal Measure rocks and so have been found over a great part of the Riding. There are of course some geological horizons where beds of ore of good quality and quantity have attracted extensive working; one such is the Tankersley Ironstone between the Silkstone and Barnsley coal seams in the middle Coal Measures,

6 P.R.O. C. 33 125 and 126.

stretching from just east of Huddersfield, twenty miles to near Sheffield. There were very extensive ironstone workings on this seam and bell pits remain as significant features of the landscape around Bentley Grange, Tankersley Park, Greaseborough, and Rawmarsh.[7] A famous Lower Coal Measure ore was that near the Halifax coals on the Lower Coal Measures near Bradford, on which the great industries of Bowling and Low Moor Iron Companies were based. In the earlier workings in places where it was not too deep, ironstone was got from bell pits, and as it occurs in nearly horizontal layers conformable with the other strata, the pits are set close together over a wide area and not aligned as are those dug along a mineral vein. Most such areas of bell pits have been levelled and built over or grassed down, but there are a few still to be seen between Wakefield and Barnsley. In the centre of Leeds the foundation excavations for buildings have from time to time laid bare groups of such pits made both for ironstone and coal. A few bell pits can be found in most parts of the Pennines but as they are now only grassed over circular mounds with a slight hollow at the centre it is difficult to date them, and they are only recognised as being for iron, coal, or lead by a geological examination of their position and spoil.

The remains of early furnaces are not very many, but there are a few forges, like Wortley near Sheffield, which has been restored and preserved.[8] Possibly the greatest effect of the early iron-making was brought about by the introduction of coppicing in the woodlands which were taken for charcoal-making. Several of these woods have continued to be regulated and are still quite an acceptable feature of the coalfield scene.

A great change came over the iron industry in the mid-

[7] A. Raistrick, 'The South Yorkshire Iron Industry', *Trans. Newcomen Society*, XIX, 1938–9, pp. 51–86.
[8] Now called Wortley Industrial Village, one of Sheffield's parks.

eighteenth century when, in Yorkshire, coke replaced charcoal as the fuel in smelting. New furnaces of larger capacity were built when coke could be got easily and where there was water power for the blowing engines. The movement was on to the river Don near Rotherham and then along the river bank sites up to Sheffield. The Calder was being claimed by the expanding textile industry and so the main part of the iron making was forced into its own new area. The Sheffield cutlers used the best steel, but much of it was imported from Sweden and the principal output of the local furnaces was wanted for wire for the wool-comb makers, rod iron for many new uses, pots, pans and other domestic articles, and massive castings like anvils, hammers, and engine parts. The cast iron from the furnace had to be converted to usable wrought iron in a forge and many of these remained at work on the side streams. It was only after Huntsman's invention of a cast steel process, and where water-wheels could operate their hammers, that steel-making spread gradually among the Sheffield iron works.

As the Industrial Revolution got under way with its ever increasing demands for iron, the furnaces were increased in individual size and grouped in twos and threes. The forging section of the industry was brought away from the out-lying streamside forges, and with rolling mills, was incorporated into the new and much larger ironworks units. Only an occasional well-established forge like Kirkstall, which had grown from a monastic origin was able to develop as a forge on a modern scale, bringing in its raw iron from the newly created furnace centres.

Along the banks of the Don from Rotherham up to Sheffield there was a rapid spread of iron and steel works and before the end of the eighteenth century ironworks had spread also from Rotherham to Masborough, providing the outline of what in the nineteenth century was to become an almost continuous mass of works engaged in the production of iron and steel. As the works grew rapidly in the nineteenth century the problem of housing the workers was responsible for the huge building programme which produced Attercliffe, Brightside and the wilderness of tightly-packed rows of minumum standard housing, the clearance of which is a feature and problem of the present generation of local government planning.

The furnaces and casting floors with ore stacks and iron stock yards were at first in the open air and then as they and their associated machinery of forge and processing departments expanded, giant cranes had their own steel-framed gantries and everything was solidly founded on the ground. The only buildings required for all this were intended not to carry loads but only to keep out the rain and wind and the typical building developed for this purpose was a gigantic non-load-bearing shed, for which the industry's own miracle materials, corrugated iron sheeting and slender steel framing were ideal. From Sheffield to Masborough there are no buildings of finely masoned stone like the great mills and warehouses of the textile area, only what appears to the rail traveller to be a never-ending procession of black corrugated iron buildings of surprising size. Gaps in the walls serving for light and ventilation give passing glimpses of glaring furnace mouths set in a Stygian darkness. Above the sheds there rises a forest of slender steel chimneys almost beyond counting, until one longs for the sight of a substantial stone chimney of the textile belt. Railway lines seem to run everywhere and shunting engines fuss about providing almost the only movement to be seen. The glow of fires, escaping steam and smoke and what appear to be acres of black corrugated iron, make this fantastic landscape, once seen, never to be confused with that of any other industry.

Stone is abundant and of more than one type. In the

north-west some of the strata below the Carboniferous Limestone provide excellent road stones and carry a thriving present-day industry, as well as having been worked for two centuries in the past. In both the Carboniferous Limestone and the Yoredale Series the limestones have been worked from before the seventeenth century for burning to lime, at first on a small scale but within the last seventy years concentrating more and more into very large-scale production units in one or two special areas. The Yoredale Series includes sandstones, some of which have provided building stone, flags and roofing slates, for the great rebuilding of the seventeenth and eighteenth centuries, but this was generally on a small scale from very numerous local quarries. The largest quarries have been on the outcrops of the more massive sandstones such as the Rough Rock in the Millstone Grit and the Gaisby Rock and Elland Flags and some other of the Lower Coal Measures. Special rocks in this group are the ganisters used as refractories in steel furnaces and the fine grindstones and millstones used in the Sheffield industry and also exported.

Parts of the Magnesian Limestone have been quarried on a fairly large scale from mediaeval times as a valuable building stone. Quarries at Thevedale near Tadcaster and Huddlestone near Sherburn in Elmet were the subject of leases for getting stone for the building of York Minster and many other mediaeval churches, so that by the fourteenth and fifteenth century not less than five monastic groups were working quarries at these two places. Traces of their work is still to be seen in overgrown quarries, and the roads by which stone was carried in wains or on sledges to the river Wharfe at Cawood or Tadcaster, for river transport, are now incorporated in modern roads, though the name of the one to Cawood, Bishopdike Road, reminds us of the great monastic estates and usage of this way. There has been much small-scale quarrying of this rock for churches and halls along the whole run of its outcrop, and occasionally it has been burned for lime. The modern quarrying is largely for refractories used in the basic hearth steel furnaces.

One of the greatest of the quarry areas, where much of the landscape has been produced by the quarries, is the area around Keighley, Leeds, and west of Bradford, Halifax, and Huddersfield, where scores of quarries have worked the Millstone Grit and the famous Gaisby Rock, Elland Flags and Oakenshaw Rock of Lower Coal Measures, with some other sandstones in the Middle Coal Measures. This extensive industry grew with the great housing and mill demands of the end of the eighteenth and early nineteenth century in which Bradford, Leeds, Halifax, Huddersfield and most of the textile towns were greatly extended, and when railway works, stations and bridges were calling for fine quality stone. One demand on the heavier rock was for engine bases, the early steam engines in the factories demanding massive stonework for their foundations. The growth of the multistorey mills and warehouses also called for fine ashlar work and the best quality cut masonry in great quantity. From the Millstone Grit quarries in particular a stone was got which was very resistant to sea water erosion, and a great export of such rock was made for underwater, along with Gaisby Rock for above-water, works, such as for the dock and harbour works at Bombay, Calcutta, Hong Kong, Sydney, Copenhagen and many other of the world's ports. Halifax stone for fine building was sent to London to build the Post Office Savings Bank, the War Office (1906), and the extensions to the British Museum (1907) among others. The Halifax flags paved many city streets and made many staircases in this country. Bradford stone was used for Woolwich Arsenal buildings and for Portsmouth Admiralty Docks in 1900.

All this meant that the quarry industry was in a boom

state through most of the nineteenth century and its remains
are fresh, and some of the quarries are still in work. The
quarries were mainly to the west of the larger towns or
around them, so some small hamlets grew into quarry
villages. Outside Thornton near Bradford, amidst a group
of quarries there is Egypt and Thornton Heights, both
created almost entirely by quarry workers. They are clusters
of well-built small cottages with substantial stone roofs,
fine flagged floors and often with garden fences made of
very large flags set on edge. Northowram (Fig. 11) and
Southowram were places where the quarries took over
much of the township fields and provided the dominating
occupation. Today the villages like Northowram are
tucked in among tips of quarry refuse and of quarries, some
of great depth, far too many to be filled in. To the west of
Elland, the village of Greetland has its quarry outlier at
Greetland Wall where quarries still produce fine stone for
municipal buildings, statuary plinths and other architectural
uses. This belt of quarry landscape stretches from Keighley,
through Denholme and then west of Halifax to the moors
west of Huddersfield. Hardly any part of this except Oven-
den Moor is free of quarries and quarry spoil heaps, of
good stone building in the hamlets, fine walled and often
paved roads from the quarries. Deep cuttings for the roads
often have retaining walls of massive size such as those near
Egypt called for their size the 'Walls of Jericho'; Masons'
Arms, Quarry Arms and so on are frequent public house
signs.

In Ribblesdale above Settle there is a new quarry landscape. Small older quarries in the pre-Carboniferous
Coniston Grits at Helwith Bridge have been lost under
several large modern quarries with output over 200,000
tons a year—with large tips, extensive crushing plants and
a never ceasing procession of heavy lorries carrying away
road ballast, limestone, and concrete aggregates to the many

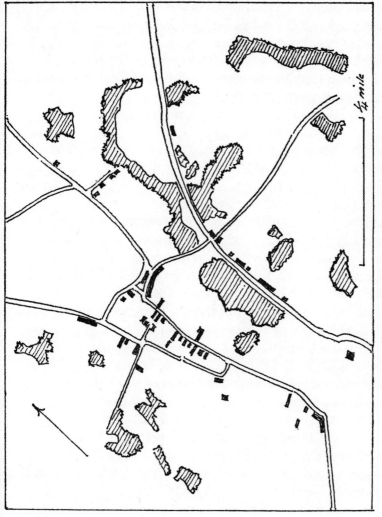

Fig. 11. Quarries at Northowram near Halifax.

new road-building projects. Two miles further up the dale at Horton in Ribblesdale, one of the largest lime-burning and crushing quarries, now worked by I.C.I. has its crushing and sorting plant and its bank of kilns but retains its railway sidings so that not all its products travel by road. The Settle to Carlisle railway line carries passengers alongside all this quarry development and past a further large-scale limestone quarry at Ribblehead Station. This is the modern landscape with high standing crushing and handling plant and huge quarry faces.

The last among the old established extractive industries which have their own landscape, is that of coal-mining. Most of the coal-working was been underground and has left as its principal recognisable feature the pit heaps, the only exception being the recent development of open-cast mining, limited in extent and temporary in its disturbance of the surface. Apart from some small-scale working of the thin coals in the Yoredale Series and Millstone Grits the mining has been in the main area of the exposed coal-field until the latter part of the nineteenth century when the eastward move to the part of the Coal Measures which dip below the later strata and which form the concealed coal-field took place. Garsdale Common, between Dentdale and Garsdale in the extreme north-west of the Riding is exceptional in having an area of about one square mile occupied by a pattern of regularly spaced coal shafts, working a seam about twenty to thirty feet below the surface. The area is now one of green roads linking these many grass-grown pit heaps with the Coal Road, and of great numbers of small pit mounds to be seen on every side.

In the true coalfield the earlier pits were set along the western edge of the field where the seams were dipping to depths of not more than a few hundred feet, and where collieries were sunk on to relatively small leases. From Bradford, by Halifax, Huddersfield, and Penistone to

Plate 21   Mouth of the Standedge Tunnel at Marsden, highest point of the Sir John Ramsden Canal.

C. H. Wood

Plate 22 Skipton. The High Street with the church and castle at the top, and early terraces filling in the former long gardens behind the High Street houses. Middletown Ward is on the bottom right hand with close-set industrial terrace housing. Millfields, top left, Leeds and Liverpool Canal in the

Bertram Unne

Plate 23 Ripon Market. Some of this area has been taken for car parking and the number of stalls is now reduced.

G. D. Bolton

Plate 24 Buckstones Moss from the Denshaw to Huddersfield road. Typical of the wide range of moors within easy reach of all the industrial towns of the West Riding. Quarry spoil heap in the bottom right corner shows we are in the area of extensive building stone quarries.

Sheffield, the collieries were remarkably numerous, just to the east of the stone-quarrying belt. Many pits were actually within the towns and for a time in the nineteenth century their pit heaps and winding gear made prominent features. Most of these heaps have now been levelled and are covered by the housing areas of the town suburbs. By 1880 the whole belt of the coalfield west of a line approximately from Bawtry by Rotherham to Leeds was covered with a close-set pattern of collieries. At first the roads had dominated a land-sale structure of the industry, but canal and later rail transport encouraged the quick expansion of the deeper pits and especially those on the thick, high quality, Barnsley and Silkstone seams. In the first twenty years of the twentieth century the pits down the eastern fringe of this zone increased rapidly in size and a wider spread of pits of still larger size appeared carrying the coal belt eastward to and just east of Doncaster. Since 1920 a number of large new collieries have been sunk in the deeper part of the concealed coalfield, almost to the line of the river Trent.

These larger nineteenth and twentieth century pits have accumulated spoil heaps big enough to be the dominant feature over miles of countryside—some of them are as much as 150 feet high and cover from fifty to a 100 acres of ground. So large are they that it is not unlikely that if accumlation were to continue at the same rate, some of them would join up into a continuous desolation. Added to this on some of the older pits, the extraction of the thick seams and the loading of the spoil heaps has produced hundreds of acres of subsidence lands now flooded. The vast flooded areas around and between collieries are sedge-grown in some cases, but in the main they are unpleasant polluted water contaminated with seeping chemicals from the encroaching spoil heaps and becoming far more unpleasant than attractive. South of Leeds a huge area of these 'flashes' extends from the very edge of the industrial sites, joining up from colliery to colliery down to and beyond Methley, a disgusting wilderness of pools, swamps and colliery spoil heaps. Only one subsidence area, that at Fairburn Ings, 618 acres, has been preserved as a bird sanctuary, being rather isolated, cleaner and much more attractive than most.

The County Planning Authority have adopted a policy which when it is carried through will materially alter for the better much of the industrial area, their intention being "to upgrade landscape . . . and to restore the potential of spoiled, degraded and waste land . . . particularly within and adjacent to, or on the fringes of, the built-up areas of the textile, steel, and coal zones." All will wish the county well in this valiant policy.[9]

The newest extractive industry to create definite changes in the general landscape is the essentially recent taking of gravel and sand for the building and engineering industries. Gravel of varying grades and qualities along with sand is being taken in large quantities from the wide spreads of river terrace gravels and glacial sands and gravels which are of fairly wide occurrence. Around Doncaster and to Retford in Nottinghamshire the floor of the Trent valley is covered with a fine quality quartzite gravel derived from the Bunter Pebble Bed of the Trias strata. The river gravels of the valleys of the Wharfe, Aire, and Calder and the large spread of glacial sands and gravels between Harrogate and Ripon are the other areas now being exploited. Of the annual production of over four million cubic yards, about half comes from around Doncaster and about a quarter each from the Ripon–Harrogate and from the three river areas. The effect on the rural landscape of this working is for a time catastrophic. The relatively thin cover of gravel is ripped out of very wide areas of scores or even hundreds of acres of rich meadow land, using great drag chain excavators

[9] *Op. cit.,* 'A growth policy for the North', 1966.

Dumps of gravel are piled around ugly washing and grading plants and the gravel workings are left as flooded areas being always below the local water table. When extraction is completed, at the best a series of huge lagoons is left which by judicious planting and landscaping can make a watersports park. At worst these derelict pools become tipping grounds for ashes and refuse in the hope eventually of restoring a land surface. Demand for these gravels is growing and this exchange of the attractive, high quality, agricultural landscape of the riverside meadows is going on at an increasing rate, creating the artificial lagoons which can only provide recreational use for a limited number of people. The alternative of crushed rock aggregates and sand is slow to reduce the demand for the easier-got and cheaper natural gravels, but the substitution will have to be faced if some of our finest agricultural areas are not to be swamped under derelict water pools.

BIBLIOGRAPHY

Bischoff, *History of Woollen and Worsted Manufactures*, 1842, reprint 1968.
Crump, W. B. *The Little Hill Farm*, 1951.
Emmison, F. G. *Types of Commonfield Parish*, London, 1965.
Finberg, J. *Exploring Villages*, London, 1958.
Young, A. *A Six Months tour through the North of England*, 3 vols. London, 1770.
Heaton, H. *The Yorkshire Woollen and Worsted Industries*, 1920.

6. Landscape of the Industrial Revolution: II

Transport: roads, canals, rail. New industrial towns.
Town services: reservoirs, etc.

THE INDUSTRIAL REVOLUTION was possible only when goods and raw materials could be moved easily between the producing areas and markets and to and from ports for import and export. The development of adequate transport facilities cannot be separated from the growth of the larger industries of textiles, iron, steel and coal, nor can a profitable discussion be based upon whether industry caused the transport revolution or whether changing transport altered the way of life of the community. Industry and transport are inseparably intermixed as the ingredients of one great complex event and it is only in an attempt at clarity that I separate them thus artificially.

The story of transport in the West Riding is the story of a changing economy and has little real existence apart from the developing needs of communities and of their gradual involvement in trade. The part played by the Roman roads in the basic settlement of the plains has been mentioned. During the Middle Ages the developing market towns were the nodes between which a network of tracks grew into a pattern of roads. Food, carried on pack-horses, was the principal commodity being moved, but a later traffic was already foreshadowed as some of the monasteries in the thirteenth century began to bring wool from their upland granges in large quantities. For this they obtained wayleaves along which not only wool moved but cattle, food, and officials also and a busy two-way usage was soon established. Roads and bridges were made between granges and monastery and between monasteries and the mediaeval markets such as Boston and York. Some of these ways were used by wagons and were roads in a rather larger sense than were the pack-horse tracks.

Alongside the wool trade there was from the twelfth century the developing trade in lead which, like the wool, was in a large part sent to distant parts of the country or even abroad. Wines, dyes, and medicaments, and articles of luxury shared in the import trades, and all these together demanded ports to some of which a difficult journey could be eased by river carriage. Lead from the Pennines was carried by land to Boroughbridge and then by boat to York or Hull for sea carriage to London or to the Continent. Roads or tracks were developed leading to the lower reaches of the rivers and to the Humber estuary. An export trade, although confined to a few special communities, had begun. The carriage of stone for York Minster helped to establish Cawood and Tadcaster for a time as river ports, while Airmyn and Boroughbridge were new villages created for the purpose of the river trade.

After the dissolution of the monasteries the change in orientation of the wool trade which was marked by the growth of Halifax, Wakefield, and Barnsley as inland wool centres, was accompanied by a new and greater network of pack-horse tracks which by the end of the sixteenth century had covered all the Pennine part of the Riding. Long stretches of these tracks are paved across soft ground with a single line of big flagstones and remain as a frequent feature in the moorland scene. The crests of the steeper valley sides are cut by the multiple furrows of these roads, cut deep by wear, abandoned for another, and made permanent by the run off of two or three centuries of heavy rainstorms. Along these tracks the 'broggers' and woolmen maintained a steady drainage of wool from the scattered farms and villages of the whole upland area into the new clothing centres, and clothiers forged the greater links between these and the rising cloth markets such as Leeds. Wool and the finished cloth were both suited to the small packs of this carrying trade, one or two packs or pieces to a horse, making a total of not more than two and a half hundredweights. It was with the development of the iron industry, the new demands for great quantities of fuel, much heavier loads and quicker carriage that the pack-horse roads became inadquate. A developing export trade directed an increasing bulk of traffic towards York and Hull and so it was inevitable that attention was more and more focused on the lower reaches of the rivers as the means of making part of the longer journeys which were now necessitated.

If we consider the transport demands of the West Riding, four areas were coming under increasing pressure for quicker outlets for goods and produce. In the north part of the Riding, the agricultural producers of Nidderdale and the richer agricultural land around Ripon and Knaresborough were seeking better transport to the great market at York and they looked to the improvement of the rivers Ouse, Nidd, and Ure as the possible answer to their problem, at least in part. The growing district which centred its marketing on Leeds saw the improvement of the Aire as a ready way to either York or Hull. The whole Calder basin was rapidly expanding its textile industry and by the improvement of the Calder to its junction with the Aire could share with Leeds in an improved water connection with Hull. Barnsley, seeking a greater outlet for its coal, looked to the Dearne, and Sheffield for its iron and steel thought in terms of an improved Don. Thus, in the late seventeenth and early eighteenth century thoughts were everywhere being turned to the improvement of river navigation and the advantages of water transport. Into these ideas the canals in the last quarter of the eighteenth century came as a natural solution, making regional links by water transport possible.

Some minor river improvement had been made before the seventeenth century but the first major scheme involving river control was the one carried through by Cornelius Vermuyden between 1626 and 1629. This, as part of the plan to drain the Hatfield Marshes, created the new course for the river Don known as the Dutch River.[1] When the flow of the Don was fairly normal small boats could use it from the Ouse as far as Barnby Dun and for about three-quarters of the year they could get even as far as Doncaster. A thriving river route at the same time was down the river Idle from Bawtry into the Trent and so to Hull. All these routes were only serviceable after a comparatively long overland carriage of the goods to the point of shipment.

From very early times the Ouse had been used from an embarkation point just below Boroughbridge for goods travelling to York and Hull and many schemes had attempted to improve this river, keep it free of shallows and control its flow. It was not, however, until the last years of the seventeenth century that the experience gained in all these minor schemes was put to the fullest use in a grand river navigation. In the sixteenth and early seventeenth centuries Halifax and Wakefield had become the new centres of the textile industries, but Leeds was fast developing as the centre for cloth finishing and dyeing, and merchants were more and more making it the market centre for finished cloth. Great amounts of cloth were coming into both Leeds and Wakefield, carried on horseback from Halifax and the weaving areas, and both towns were looking for ways of economising on the heavy charge of the next stage, carriage to Hull. From their joint deliberations

[1] S. Smiles, *Lives of the Engineers*, 1862, I, p. 36 ff.

Leeds and Wakefield in 1689 sought and obtained an Act "For making and keeping navigable the Rivers of Aire and Calder . . .". The rivers Aire and Calder were to be improved from below their junction, a place called Weeland, up to the two towns of Leeds and Wakefield, so as to allow of the easy passage of "barges, boats, lighters and other vessels".[2] The preamble to the Act claims that this work would be a great advantage to the clothing trade, and would advance the trade and commerce of market towns and all places near to the rivers, and the increase of watermen would lead to "the extraordinary preservation of the Highways", we presume by lessening their use. The Proprietors were to clean, enlarge, and straighten the river course, to make cuts through adjacent lands to cut off bends, with power to pull down corn mills, weirs, fulling mills (with ample compensation clauses), make towing paths and do all that may be required to make a perfectly navigable passage on the two rivers. This work was carried out and quickly proved its worth: By 1774, however, it was seen that the lower course of the Aire between the end of the Aire and Calder Navigation and the Ouse was difficult to control without vast works, so the two corporations secured an Act to make "a navigable Canal from the said river Aire, from Weeland to the river Ouze . . . from Haddesley, to the river Ouze at the Old Brook Garth at Ouze Gate End, within the township of Selby".[3]

When goods were carried from Leeds by pack-horse and waggon Selby was the nearest point on the river Ouse and the greater part of the trade was carried there for transhipment to boats going down the Ouse and Humber to Hull or up the river to York. The improvement of the lower Aire by the Aire and Calder Navigation took most of this

---

[2] 10 & 11 William III (1698) and 14 George III (1774).

[3] B. F. Duckham, *The Yorkshire Ouse*, 1967, pp. 70–77. *Ibid.*, 'Selby and the Aire and Calder Navigation', *Journal of Transport History*, VII, 2, 1965.

trade away from Selby to the little town of Airmyn at the junction of the Aire and Ouse, and eight miles lower down the river Ouse. This seemed to be the beginning of a complete decline of Selby. For seventy years the Aire and Calder Navigation carried nearly all the traffic on the lower Aire and the great increase in volume may be realised from the rise in the rent of the tolls on this portion of river from £800 a year in 1704 to £8500 in 1774, this last figure being estimated by some as being far below the actual value. The lower course, however, was very difficult to maintain and after much opposition the Proprietors got the Act of 1774 which enabled them to cut a canal from the nearest point of the Aire at Haddesley, to Selby, a distance of little more than five miles. A small estate of eight acres was bought in Selby and wharves, dry dock, warehouses and offices were built for a rapidly expanding trade. The general features of the town, the expansion of the flour milling, provender, and shipbuilding industries, largely stem from the relatively short period of great prosperity brought by the Aire and Selby Canal.

The docks of the Aire and Calder Canal became the focal point of rapid growth and an industrial and transport section was built with more or less success on to the older part of the town. The industries which quickly grew up around the docks and created the impressive buildings which are still a characteristic of the area, were flour milling, and the extraction of vegetable oils and fats. Today the town is an important centre for the manufacture of cattle foods and provender of all kinds. Shipbuilding has provided an interesting part of the riverside aspect of the town. The market and the general prosperity were also helped considerably by the bridge across the Ouse, built in 1792. This is a timber bridge with a swinging section to allow the passage of river traffic. It is a toll bridge and protracted negotiations for the extinction of the tolls have been a

feature of the municipal life of the town for a very long
time.[4]

Before 1820 a branch Customs House was built in Selby
and from 1780 for the next fifty years Selby was the starting
point for a rapidly increasing passenger traffic on the river.
The bridge had brought many turnpikes to this point and
coach services developed from the West Riding as well as
from the east side of the Ouse. There were twenty-eight
hotels, inns, and taverns for travellers and market visitors,
and these affected the appearance of the streets and brought
trade to the town which was described in 1822 as "a brisk
market town". Coaches were scheduled to run in connection with Steam Packet services to Hull after 1815. This
period of prosperity is marked by some very good Georgian
building in the main streets.

With the increasing bulk of traffic, however, the Selby–
Aire Canal was found to be too shallow to allow its use by
larger boats and new proposals were made which offered
a serious threat to Selby's position. The collieries around
Barnsley and in south Yorkshire were rapidly increasing
their output in the early decades of the nineteenth century
and were finding land transport slow, expensive and incapable of dealing with the new scale of production. The
industry turned more and more to the attractions of water
transport which would carry their output direct to the
Humber estuary. Attempts to improve the Don navigation had been frequent and persistent but equally persistent was the opposition of Doncaster, Pontefract and in
particular, the ship-masters on the Trent who carried
much trade from a wide area of south Yorkshire collected
at Bawtry.

The first effort of Barnsley was by way of the Barnsley
Canal, running nearly north to join the Aire and Calder

[4] Plans are now being studied for new transport lines at Selby, including a
new bridge.

Navigation at Heath on the Calder, on the outskirts of Wakefield. The journey was then easy by the Selby Canal to Selby, and for a time a large amount of coal was taken this way and then up the Ouse to York where it became a serious rival to coal from Newcastle which came by coaster to Hull then by the Ouse lighters to York. The Barnsley Canal was operating during the first decade of the nineteenth century and about the same time another canal was constructed, the Dearne and Dove Canal which gave water transport from the Barnsley collieries to the Don at Swinton Bridge and then by the Don and the Dutch River to an outlet on the Ouse at Old Goole. The making of these two waterways gave a great impetus to the development of new and larger collieries on the wide district of the coalfield which was underlain by the famous Barnsley seam and in part by the Silkstone coal.

The lower course of the Aire was becoming more inefficient and incapable of carrying any larger boats than those used in the original Aire and Calder scheme, so that in 1819 the Aire and Calder Navigation Proprietors surveyed a line for a direct canal from Knottingley, fourteen miles below Leeds, to the outlet of the Dutch River on the Ouse at Goole, about nine miles below Selby. This would not only cut out the lower Aire which was so difficult to control, but would also cut out the dangerous bends at Kilpin and near Barlow on the Ouse between Goole and Selby. Land near the mouth of the Dutch River and on the north side of its outfall was purchased and warped and the new Knottingley to Goole Canal, for its last five miles was made alongside the Dutch River to docks which became the nucleus of a new town.[5]

Goole, therefore, is a purpose-built town of nineteenth century origin and growth. Here are the docks for sea-going traffic and the great lock gates of the inland canals,

[5] B. F. Duckham, *The Yorkshire Ouse*, 1967, pp. 86–114.

warehouses and offices, Customs House and inns, backed by a town of planned streets (Plate 17). The streets are very wide with many attractive terraces of houses ranging from small houses for labourers to larger houses for traders and merchants. Aire Street is one such fine terrace of well designed houses, though the ground floor of nearly all of them is now converted to shop premises. A fine Georgian inn is still a feature of the street. The large warehouses built for the canal about 1826 are 160 feet long by eighty feet and sixty feet wide respectively and six storeys high. The docks and town were built by a firm of civil engineers and contractors, Jolliffe and Banks, with Woodhead and Hurst, architects of Doncaster, designing most of the buildings. Goole is thus in the greater part a canal and port town of unified design and is a notable piece of industrial architecture. With the attraction of railways to the docks, Goole grew and is now Yorkshire's third greatest port, with a population of almost 19,000.

Before 1770 a proposal was made for a trans-Pennine canal to be a link between the east and west coasts. A canal was proposed to be made from Leeds to Liverpool which, with the Aire and Calder Canal would give the textile areas an outlet to either sea. This canal was authorised by an Act in 1769 "for making and maintaining a Navigable cut or canal from Leeds Bridge . . . to the North Ladys Walk in Liverpool and from thence to the river Mersey . . . will also tend to the improvement of the adjacent Lands, Relief of the Poor, and the Preservation of the Public Roads, and moreover be of great Utility . . .". The boats were to be sixty feet long and fourteen feet wide of forty to fifty tons burthen and so able to travel from Liverpool to Hull without any transhipment of cargo. It would not require more than six or seven days to pass from Liverpool to Hull at a charge of twenty-three shillings per ton. The chief products to pass along it were estimated as likely to be coal, limestone, and stone, corn and general merchandise.[6] In 1774 it was opened from Liverpool to Wigan and by 1776 to Burnley. The final connection was not made across the watershed to the Yorkshire section at Gargrave until 1816.

Although the Leeds and Liverpool Canal encouraged the development of industry around Leeds and through all Airedale, it was of no outstanding value to the textile area in and around the Calder valley. With the opening of the Aire and Calder Navigation, cloth was carried from Halifax to either Leeds or Wakefield. Halifax, perched on the hillsides of a very deep and narrow valley sent and brought its goods by a mountainous road across Swales Moor, eight miles to Bradford and then a further eight miles to Leeds, or else by an equally difficult road sixteen miles to Wakefield. In 1757 a canal was surveyed by the Yorkshire engineer John Smeaton to extend the Aire and Calder from Wakefield to Halifax, but the situation of Halifax was such that the canal terminus was made at Salterhebble, still leaving two miles of heavy haulage into the town. This canal, the Calder and Salterhebble Canal was made between 1758 and 1765. A branch canal was taken forward along the side of the Calder as far as Sowerby Bridge where the wharves became the commercial centre of the new town with Wharfe Street as its principal road. This canal was completed by 1767 but was soon wrecked by a disastrous flood. It was reconstructed by Smeaton.

The success of the Leeds and Liverpool Canal convinced the Lancashire manufacturers and traders of the value of a trans-Pennine connection with Yorkshire, and the Rochdale Canal via the Todmorden gorge at the head of the Calder was planned. This connection was made by the Rochdale Canal between Rochdale and Sowerby Bridge in 1802.[7]

[6] John Hustler, *An explanation of the plan of the Canal from Leeds to Liverpool* . . . etc.
[7] C. Hadfield, *British Canals*, 1966, map, p. 152, etc.

In 1828 the Calder and Salterhebble Canal was extended the two miles into Halifax at Bailey Hall which then rapidly expanded into the town's main industrial centre.

Some idea of the effect of the canals can be got from the advertising connected with transport in the year 1822. From Leeds, the Aire and Calder Company's fly boats went to Selby every evening except Sunday. The journey took twelve hours and cargoes were next morning put on board a steam packet which arrived in Hull the same afternoon and were carried from there to London. The Company also had 'contract' boats which carried regular freight to London, Lynn, Wisbech, Boston, Yarmouth, Newcastle, and other coastal towns. Inland vessels went to York, Malton, Gainsborough, Lincoln, and many other places. They had "about 40 vessels in the transporting of goods on the canal" to all places between Leeds and Liverpool. There were at least ten other companies with fly boats and contract boats some of them offering carriage 'in one bottom' to wharves in London. From Halifax "Messrs Milnes, contract vessels go weekly from Salterhebble to St Catherine's Wharfe, London; agents B. Milnes, Silver Street, Halifax, and J. Milnes, London." Similar notices refer to eleven other firms of carriers whose boats from Salterhebble or Sowerby Bridge carried to Hull, Wakefield, Liverpool, Sheffield, Rotherham, Gainsborough, and Manchester on daily or on particular day schedules as well as connecting with London. In 1780 Huddersfield had a short canal extension, Sir John Ramsden's Navigation from the Aire and Calder, and could offer daily service to Manchester, "whence packages are forwarded to all parts of the kingdom". This of course used the Rochdale Canal. Others offered daily services to all parts by way of Hull.[8]

[8] E. Baines, *History, Directory and Gazeteer of the County of Yorkshire*, Vol. I, 'West Riding', 1822.

W. White, *Directory of Leeds, Bradford . . . and the Clothing Districts of the West Riding of Yorkshire*, 1847.

This new transport was of tremendous value to the textile areas but the iron and steel district around Sheffield was not so fortunate. The navigation of the river Don had been a subject of constant dispute from an early date. When the tides were full it was possible for small boats to get up the river as far as Barnby Dun or even to Doncaster, but all suggestions for its improvement to take larger boats were opposed by Doncaster and Pontefract in fear that their trade would be diminished; Bawtry and Gainsborough claimed that the opening of the Don would reduce their trade down the Trent and other objectors thought that locks would impede the drainage and weirs for water-wheels would have to be destroyed. Sheffield with its growing trade of over £50,000 for export, and as much as 4,500 tons of lead from nearby Derbyshire, had to send goods overland to Bawtry. Land carriage to Doncaster had risen to between 13,000 and 14,000 tons to be sent forward by water carriage.

In 1726 the Company of Cutlers decided to make the Don navigable for boats of twenty tons, from Holmstile in Doncaster to Tinsley, with a good road from Tinsley to Sheffield, and so bring water carriage within three miles of the centre of the town.[9] The Don Navigation became more important to the Sheffield district in the nineteenth century when it was carried into Sheffield in 1819, and when the lower course was in part shortened by the New Junction Canal from Kirk Bramwith to the Aire and Calder Canal, and by the Stainforth and Keadby Canal from the same place on the Don across to Keadby near Scunthorpe on the Trent. These two routes took the shipping to Goole or to Hull (Plate 18).

All this network of canals across the industrial valleys has resulted in a special landscape, that of the towpaths in the more rural districts along the Leeds and Liverpool and

[9] T. S. Willan, *Early History of the Don Navigation*, 1965.

along other canals, with locks and lock-keepers' houses. There are a few spectacular canal landscapes. Near Bingley, the Leeds and Liverpool crosses the Aire on the 'Seven Arches' aqueduct, and climbs by the famous one, two, three and five rise locks in rapid succession (Plate 19). The long miles of the Dutch River and the Knottingley and Goole Canal, in their parallel run are unique, while the course of the Rochdale Canal through the deep Pennine passes provides an exciting journey. In the towns, warehouses, wharves and offices are often excellent buildings, and as we shall see later, the canals have attracted the mills and factories to their banks, so that through the towns and cities, the canal is walled almost the whole length by mills and industrial buildings on both sides.

The success of the canal transport was intimately connected with, and in some ways indebted to the slightly earlier and the contemporary development of turnpike roads. Just befor the canal period some important Turnpike Trusts were formed, such as that which was responsible for the Kendal to Keighley road. This was formed via Skipton and Kirkby Lonsdale to connect Kendal with Keighley and then by the Keighley to Halifax Turnpike, forward to Halifax. The prime purpose of this road was to speed and increase the flow of wool from Westmorland and Craven to the West Riding clothiers at Halifax market. Other roads connected Halifax with Leeds, 1740, Halifax, Bradford, and Leeds, 1742, and still earlier, Halifax and Rochdale, 1734. This last road went via Blackstone Edge, the notorious mountain route which so deeply impressed Defoe when he travelled that way a few years before the new road was made. Another wild mountain road was that from Halifax via Heptonstall, then across the moors, by the Long Causeway to Burnley. Many of these roads brought goods down to the canal wharves and particularly in the lower areas, were most important service ways used in connection with the canals.[10]

As the industries, both textile and iron, expanded and the bulk of carried material increased in proportion, larger carts and waggons found the high-level roads with their many very steep gradients more and more difficult and the example of the canals was followed in making use of the river valleys and the low-level passes. New roads were planned, often compelled by the topography to keep close alongside the canal. This movement into the valley bottoms emphasised what the canals had started, the migration of manufacturing industry from the early hillside locations into new towns on the banks of the canals and at the road bridges. When steam power began to spread the canals provided the cheapest form of transport for the large amounts of coal needed in regular supply and the canal could also supply condenser water for the engines. There were other factors which contributed to the same movement. The older hand-weaving centre of Heptonstall, high on the hill spur between the Calder and the Hepton Brook, is a clear example of two stages of migration. Following the spinning-jenny and its development into the water frame, small mills with water-wheels were set up on the Hepton Brook for spinning yarn. For finishing cloth fulling mills had long been in use and many of these had been built on the Calder, often near to older corn mills. Arkwright's invention in 1775 of the carding machine for the preparation of wool added yet another process for a water-powered mill. The small, first-generation mills on the tributary streams were soon superseded by larger mills on the main river and with the coming of steam, grouped mills, carding, spinning and fulling, and before long, weaving, were established on the canals and rivers around the places where bridges brought roads to a river crossing (Plate 20).

[10] W. B. Crump, *Huddersfield Highways down the Ages,* Tolson Museum Handbook, 1949.

Below Heptonstall mills were built at Hebden (Hepton) Bridge at and around the junction of side stream and river; Sowerby on the hill top was succeeded by Sowerby Bridge which became a canal terminus; Rastrick was followed by Brighouse (Bridge House) and so the valley bottom was filled with new industrial towns. Mills migrated down the tributary valleys so that Luddenden near Halifax was replaced by Luddenden Foot nearer the Calder. In the Colne valley many of these migrations can be recognised. Old hand-spinning and weaving centres on the opposite high slopes of the Colne valley, like Meltham and Thick Hollins, with the manor corn mill at the bridge in the valley bottom between them, soon had a scribbling (carding) mill and fulling mill added above the bridge. More and more work-people meant more and more houses and New Town grew around these valley bottom mills.

These paired village-town groups were coming throughout the textile area of the Calder drainage, and spread to a less extent into the much broader valley of the Aire. Baildon on the edge of the moors, with older weaving cottages had its new mill town at Baildon Bridge; Apperley has its complement in Apperley Bridge. A few towns were totally new creations, such as Saltaire built beyond Shipley, by Titus Salt in 1858, who built not only mills but a whole village on the banks of the Aire, with the Leeds and Liverpool Canal running between his two mills and the railway between mills and village. Ripleyville near Bowling, built for the workpeople of Ripley's big dye works and Lilycroft for Listers at Manningham, were soon absorbed into Bradford, and many other such industrial areas were specially built, though these were mainly in the mid-nineteenth century, and the projects of single individuals, the new large-scale industrialist.

Before the middle of the nineteenth century another revolution in transport was experienced, that of the railways, but although this affected the townscape by adding stations and warehouses, it had less effect on the location of settlements than road and canal had had. In fact the railways came late enough to plan their routes to meet the towns and industrial sites which were, for the most part, already settled. As with the earlier transport, the railways in the West Riding originated around the rapidly growing industries and commerce of Leeds. Before 1850 the merchanting of cloth and the ready-made clothing industries had migrated towards Leeds and Bradford and both towns were feeling the need for more rapid communications. In 1812 Leeds had seen the building of the Middleton Colliery railway with Blenkinsop's steam locomotive running into the coal staithes at Hunslet. In 1830 the Liverpool to Manchester railway trials had proved the success of this mode of transport and in 1834 the first goods and passenger railway in Yorkshire was built between Leeds and Selby. This gave Leeds businessmen a quick route, at first only an hour and a quarter, to the docks at Selby where they could join boats for Hull and London or conduct business at the port and return the same day to Leeds.[11]

During the next few years railway connections between north and south were being made and York, Durham, and Newcastle were linked together and Leeds joined to this system by its Leeds to Thirsk line in 1849. Leeds was connected to the developing Midland group at Normanton, then by Rotherham and the Rother valley to Derby and London. In the 1840's Leeds made connections by rail with Bradford and Skipton, then forward to Hellifield and Ingleton, connecting at Skipton with the Lancashire and Yorkshire Railway, thus getting a line to Manchester. Dewsbury, Huddersfield and Wakefield were all connected with Leeds during these busy years. Sheffield was not on any of the

[11] W. W. Tomlinson, *The North Eastern Railway: its rise and development*, 1875, reprint David and Charles, ed. K. Hoole, 1967, pp. 203–5 ; 254–9.

147

main lines and was rather isolated in its deep basin of hills, but in 1838 it linked with Rotherham by the Sheffield and Rotherham line, being able there to make connections with the main line south. In the last years of the 1840's Sheffield completed a line to Manchester via the very difficult Woodhead tunnels and so got a direct trans-Pennine route which became more and more important, being one of the early lines to be electrified in 1953. This Manchester to Sheffield line was continued to Lincoln in 1851.

Another cross line from Swinton to Doncaster gave access to the main line to London and northward, and a direct line was built from Swinton via Pontefract to York. At the same time the Hull and Barnsley direct line gave a quick outlet for the coal and goods from the rapidly developing Barnsley coalfield. Tunnels had been made to allow a direct line south from Sheffield to Chesterfield on the Midland line to Derby and trains were then able to run through Sheffield on the main London journey from Leeds. In 1874 Leeds was given a direct line north by the making of the Settle to Carlisle line by Ribblehead, probably the finest line in England for magnificent scenery, and a line having splendid viaducts at Ribblehead, two in Dentdale, one in Garsdale and others in the Eden valley. The Thames–Clyde express still thunders along this route.

Mills which were using steam power and those with processes such as dyeing and finishing which consumed a lot of water, built small dams or 'lodges' as part of the general mill lay-out, bringing water from a nearby stream by a culverted leat. The dam thus became a common feature of the new mill areas of the towns and many are still to be seen. The canals, particularly the trans-Pennine ones, needed great quantities of water to make up the losses incurred every time the numerous locks were filled from a higher pound—the stretch of canal between one lock and the next—and then emptied through the succession of locks to the lower level. The Rochdale Canal has a number of shallow but extensive reservoirs all along the county boundary moors between Rochdale and Todmorden, and the Leeds and Liverpool Canal has its 'make up' reservoirs for the summit level, at Winterburn on a tributary of the Aire and at Foulridge just over the Lancashire border. The Winterburn reservoir is tucked away in a valley which is off any road and only occasional ramblers and fishermen see much of it. In contrast with this the Foulridge reservoir is the location of a flourishing yachting club and every weekend it is a gay sight with yachts, and a source of pleasure and recreation to increasing numbers of people from both the West Riding and east Lancashire.

One of the most spectacular canals is that between Huddersfield and Ashton-under-Lyne. The Sir John Ramsden Canal had given Huddersfield a route into Lancashire by the Rochdale Canal but by 1794 the extraordinary difficulties of an almost direct line across the Pennines by way of Marsden, were mastered. This new canal follows the river Colne upstream for seven and a half miles and climbs to a summit level of 656 feet by means of forty-two locks. One of the spectacular feats achieved by the engineers was the driving of the Standedge Tunnel, 5451 yards long, through which the canal is carried to Saddleworth (Plate 21). After a four miles long summit level the canal descends to Stalybridge to make a junction with the Manchester to Ashton-under-Lyne Canal at Ashton in the Tame valley, using thirty-three locks for the descent. This short canal between Huddersfield and Ashton-under-Lyne climbs about 430 feet and descends over 300 feet in the course of nineteen and three-quarter miles by means of seventy-five locks and the longest canal tunnel in the country. The use of water was excessive when boats were ascending and each lock had to be filled from the pound above it, and thus necessitated the construction of seven 'make up' reservoirs on the moors around Standedge. In spite of the difficulties and high cost the canal was a great asset to Huddersfield and was very fully used.

The rapid growth of the industrial towns with the increases in population and industries created a demand for water which it was impossible to meet by springs and wells and the long period of reservoir construction began. Small reservoirs near the towns soon proved inadequate and by the third quarter of the nineteenth century whole valleys and moorland gathering grounds were being marked out as the preserves for particular towns. Leeds looked to the Washburn valley, tributary to Wharfedale; Bradford turned to Nidderdale: Halifax to the valley heads in the wide moors between it and Colne. Huddersfield had built two small reservoirs at Longwood in 1827 and 1828 and added two higher and larger ones at Wessenden and Deanhead, on the Wessenden Brook and Blackburn Brook, in 1836 and 1838, only about seven miles from the town centre. These served the town for the next thirty years, but new and greater resources were essential by 1870 and in the next few years five more reservoirs were built, the town having got the Huddersfield Waterworks Act in 1869 to authorise these constructions. Still another reservoir was built in 1937 in addition to a large number of boreholes sunk to tap the large reserves of excellent quality underground water.[12] The reservoirs of Huddersfield and Halifax and of other towns both in Yorkshire and Lancashire, along with the canal reservoirs, have, converted the quadrangle of Pennines between Burnley–Keighley–Huddersfield–Rochdale into an area where the landscape everywhere includes great stretches of water in nearly seventy reservoirs. The dominant note is a wide upland of heath and heather, some rocky crags, and one or more lakes in the headwaters of almost every stream.

[12] T. W. Woodhead, *History of the Huddersfield Water Supplies,* Tolson Museum Handbook, X, 1939.

Sheffield over the same period built thirteen reservoirs on the tributaries of the river Don and then, still short of water, joined the Derwent Water Board to build the succession of reservoirs in the Derwent valley. The Ladybower and the other reservoirs are now a valuable part of the scenery of the north part of the Peak National Park. Leeds and Bradford had to go further afield than most of their neighbours and the Bradford reservoirs in Nidderdale and the Leeds ones in the Washburn, the last one only filled in 1967, flooded the valley bottoms on a larger scale than the upper reservoirs had done. They created a new landscape in the upper part of inhabited dales where houses had to be moved and large schemes to prevent pollution, undertaken. They also involved long pipe lines for the supply, with service reservoirs and pressure towers in the town suburbs.

The limestone areas of Craven and the north-west remain free of reservoirs through the nature of the geology which allows of few watertight valleys. The needs of the scant population and the tiny villages can be met by piped springs and small service reservoirs. There is a strong hope that before the engineers and geologists have to attempt the improvement and use of these valleys, alternative sources of water, barrages and the desalination of sea water, will be commercial propositions and so some part of our valleys might be saved from the partial drowning.

BIBLIOGRAPHY

Appleton, J. H. *The Railway Network of South Yorkshire*, 1956.
Copeland, J. *Roads and their Traffic*, Newton Abbot, 1968.
Duckham, B. F. *The Yorkshire Ouse*, Newton Abbot, 1967.
Hadfield, C. *The Canal Age,* Newton Abbot, 1968.
Hadfield, C. *British Canals*, 3rd edn., Newton Abbot, 1968.
Haldane, A. R. B. *The Drove Roads of Scotland*, London, 1952.
Raistrick, A. *Green Tracks on the Pennines*, Clapham, 1962.

7. Towns and cities

The growth of towns:
Rural market towns: Skipton, Ripon. Textile towns:
Halifax, Bradford. Coal towns: Barnsley, Doncaster.
Steel towns: Sheffield, Rotherham.

A MODERN MAP of the West Riding shows up in striking fashion the conglomeration of towns and cities which make an almost continuous pattern from Sheffield in the south to Leeds in the north, covering the area between the Pennine moors and the rich farming belt of the lowland. This is the area of County and Municipal boroughs knit together by almost indistinguishable Urban Districts. Here the stranger has difficulty in deciding which town or city he is in, and here is the area where roadside town boundary signs assume a vital importance. This continuum of towns is one popular conception of the West Riding, elaborated by the addition of countless grim factories, dreary rows of houses, chimneys, smoke, grime and colliery tip-heaps.

This is a picture that might apply in part to the older industrial areas of some of the towns but it is one that is rapidly changing as new planning and rehabilitation goes forward at an increasing pace. However, it has never been a true picture even of the industrial towns, and for most of the Riding it has always been false and irrelevant. In the north-western dales the landscape is of a quality that has merited its designation as a National Park. Outside the Park area there are many other parts classed officially as Areas of Outstanding Natural Beauty (A.O.N.B.s) of which Bowland is a fine and extensive example. There is a broad zone, the length of the county on the east which is a rich agricultural landscape with attractive villages, parks and halls, which can compare with any other rural area in the country. Few critics remember that a large part of the County Borough of Sheffield lies within the Peak National Park and that Sheffield has a larger proportion of green open spaces within its boundary than any other city in Britain.

Outside the heavy industrial belt the towns are wide spaced and are primarily country market towns with a population much less than 20,000. The growth of towns in the rural areas has followed at least a fairly uniform pattern with only the local variations from town to town which one might expect, but these are enough to give each place its own distinctive character. We might look briefly at two of these rural towns, Skipton and Ripon, Skipton with a castle and market, centre for the hill farming, sheep and cattle-rearing area of Craven, and Ripon with its minster and a market, closer to the arable and dairy farms of the Vale of York. Skipton in the nineteenth century acquired industries, while Ripon grew as a commercial and residential town with the seat of a bishop, a college, and a growing market. Both became vital centres of transport and services for a very extensive rural area.[1]

At Skipton a stream, the Ellerbeck, occupies a late and post-glacial gorge which cuts through Skipton Rock, the steep ridge formed by the limestones of the core of the Skipton anticline. On emerging from this gorge the beck has built up a delta of gravels, sand, and some clay, in the edge of what, through several millennia after the Ice Age, was a glacial lake impounded behind the Cononley moraine. From the gorge the surface of these deltaic gravels slopes gently south for half a mile to the swampy meadows of the old lake alluvium. The head of the delta was chosen as a settlement site by Anglian invaders in the seventh

[1] Population in 1961, Skipton: 13,008; Ripon: 10,486.

century, but it had been used in both Bronze and Iron Age, and crossed by the Roman road from Aldborough to Ribchester. At the Norman Conquest Skipton was like all the average Anglian villages in the area, with only four carucates of land in two town field areas east and west of the village. A track from the village centre down to the river meadows became the present Sheep Street and its continuation the first part of the Keighley Road. The name of Skipton, a sheep farm, and of the neighbouring hamlet Skibden, the sheep valley, like Sheep Street, emphasises the age-long connection with sheep.

The impetus for the growth of Skipton was given after the Norman Conquest when the pre-Conquest manor of Bolton which had belonged to King Edwin, was given to the Norman de Romille, along with a large number of other manors in Yorkshire. Before 1100 Romille selected the rock at the Ellerbeck Gorge for his castle, to become the head of his new Honour of Skipton. Recent excavations have uncovered the entrance of this original castle on the west side, with a track down to the ford across Ellerbeck near the present Mill Bridge. The earliest tenements in Skipton seem to have been grouped around this ford. With the garrison and followers housed in and around the Castle a market became essential and this was established south of the Castle in the head of what is now the High Street. In the twelfth century the canons of Embassy (later Bolton Priory) were given freedom of toll in the market along with the church built between market and castle. There are the remains of a fourteenth century timber house front inside the Red Lion Inn which overlooks the market place, a few feet back from the present building line, and several other buildings show an old frontage line proving the market place to have been wider than it now is. A market cross was built at the south end and a lively market developed.

In 1379 the town had seventy-nine labourers' families and forty-eight tradesmen and craftsmen, a large proportion of them merchants and traders. These included thirteen families concerned with making or dealing in cloth, and Peter de Brabant, his son and their wives, Flemish weavers, were making shalloons. There was a corn mill and a fulling mill, inns and shops.

The growing plan can be recovered from many surveys and valuations of the Castle property, the earliest in 1311, when the properties mentioned were near the ford and the two mills. The Castle was then the centre of administration of a large forest area and the site of the Honour Courts and was a very busy place. In the fourteenth and fifteenth centuries the growth centred around the market place and along Sheep Street. The town became stabilised along the High Street leading down from the Castle and church to the line of the Roman road at the foot, the broad street being divided in its lower half by Middle Row with Sheep Street on its west side and High Street on the east. Behind the houses on the west side long gardens ran down to the Ellerbeck and on the east side similar gardens extended a comparable distance to Rectory Lane on the edge of the East field. The road approximately on the line of the Roman road crossed the High Street foot at right-angles, and became part of a very important mediaeval road between York and Lancaster. By the fifteenth century there were a few houses along this road and near the foot of High Street one of the more important ones was that of the Prior of Bolton on Swadford Street. A market was granted to the town at an early date and in 1311 it was valued in these terms "the p'fitte of the weekely m'kett and two faiers ther in the yere xvj.l. xiijs. iiijd."

The basic plan of the town was now stabilised, its simplest form being an I, two roughly parallel east–west roads with a short north to south link which was the High Street.

The north road was from Knaresborough by Bolton, through Skipton and on to the north-west; the southern road came from Harewood and Otley to Skipton and west to Clitheroe and Lancashire. The Castle and church were on the east–west road at the top of the High Street, and the foot of the town was a very slight expansion along the two arms of the southern road. Shops lined the High Street, the wide northern half of which was the market place. In 1652 there were, on the Clifford rent roll, more than forty houses and cottages, seventeen shops, and forty-six other tenants and closes, houses, or other properties, including a fulling mill and a dyehouse (Plate 22).

Through the seventeenth century the life of the town focused on Castle and market, an extended charter for a fair which was described as "very useful to those living within forty miles near the aforesaid town, for the buying, selling and exhibition of horses, cows, bullocks, and sheep", having been granted in 1597. This fair was to be held every second Tuesday from Easter to Christmas. In 1756 there were ten additional fairs besides the one just mentioned and all these with the weekly market confirmed the character of Skipton as a growing market town. There was a steady increase in the sale of corn and with the deforesting of Knaresborough Forest and the increase of corn land there, the New market (now Newmarket Street) became an important corn market for a very wide area where arable town fields were being enclosed for stock feeding, and corn growing was becoming obsolete. The seventeenth century was a time of prosperity and many, if not most, of the properties in the High Street were then rebuilt in stone. The Castle which had been somewhat ruinous was rebuilt by Lady Anne Clifford in the years following 1655.

The eighteenth century saw a little expansion of the town mainly along Swadford Street and Newmarket Street, the crossroads at the town foot, where, between 1717 and 1725, leases were granted to wool combers and weavers to build cottages, and a few years later further cottages were built for both shalloon and worsted weavers, thus making a small industrial corner to the town. In 1753 the Keighley to Kendal Turnpike, which passed through Skipton, was designed to help the trade in wool between Westmorland and Halifax, and it stabilised the trade and made Skipton a gathering centre for Craven wool. The Malham Moor fair for Highland cattle stimulated the graziers of Craven and boosted Skipton to an important cattle market. In 1774 the Yorkshire section of the Leeds and Liverpool Canal reached the town and began what was the greatest period of change. There is no doubt that throughout the eighteenth century Skipton was above everything else, a market and commercial centre for an increasing rural area. As the arable farming was displaced by cattle feeding and breeding over the Craven highlands and dairy farming over the lowlands, Skipton shops and markets became the essential heart of the area. The chief mark on the town was the Georgian refronting and extension of the High Street houses, and the filling out and completion of Swadford and Newmarket Streets.

The canal for some time was primarily concerned with limestone, manure, and food. A short branch, the Springs Canal, was cut alongside the Ellerbeck to a position behind the Castle to which terminus limestone was brought by a tramway from quarries opened just to the east on the Skipton Rock in Haw Park, an old park of the Castle. The limestone was carried on the canal towards Leeds and Bradford in the Millstone Grit and Coal Measure areas, and burned in limekilns on the canal side which were served with coal from the coalfield. The burned lime was used only partly in the developing building trade, and mainly in the improvement of the poorer soils around the towns. A note in 1774 says that there were then forty kilns at work on the canal side between Skipton and Bradford. The promoters of the canal estimated that they would have considerable tolls on yarn, woollens, linen, and other goods between Skipton and Bradford and this expectation proved to be true for a while. None the less, one of the earliest mills in Skipton, the High Mill, near the Castle, was built and opened in 1785 as a cotton spinning mill. It was, however, the worsted industry which developed in the town and the area which it served, and a report in 1793 speaks of a large house employed in sorting and combing wool and using 3000 packs a year. It was used in mills in the region, spun and made into shalloons, etc. and the noils (short fibres) were sent to Dewsbury and Rochdale.

A fairly widespread worsted industry in Craven was gradually concentrated on Skipton in the early nineteenth century, as the demands for larger mills and more power could only be met where the steam engine could be brought into use. The canal was ideal for the transport of coal in bulk and in the second quarter of the century the canal banks were lined with new mills and weaving sheds. The growth of industry demanded an increasing labour force with all its problems of housing, schools, services, and other town amenities. The growth of population caused a housing shortage which more than once reached acute proportions. Relief from overcrowding in the later decades of the eighteenth century and the early nineteenth century was only obtained by the sacrifice, at high prices, of the long gardens that lay behind the old houses of the High Street, running on the west down to Ellerbeck, and on the east to the Old Court Lane and Rectory Lane. Along these long, narrow gardens rows of small houses were built at right angles to the High Street and the process of consolidation of the town centre was carried a long way. By 1830 the town had acquired a new feature, the numerous 'yards' which open between the shops of the High Street and run back as narrow tunnels to open into a long and very narrow alleyway, with houses down one side, and usually the blank back wall of the houses of the next yard on the other. All the stories of "defence from the Scots raiders" and other romantic nonsense told about them can be dismissed: their origin is much more practical. With few exceptions they were pleasant gardens for two centuries after the last raid. There are, however, a few buildings of the late seventeenth century in one or two of the yards, but these are only the isolated first foreshadowing of the later infilling.

In 1829 the Dewhirst brothers built a new mill near the canal and moved from the small water-powered factories they had been operating in some of the dales villages. They had steam power and began spinning and weaving worsteds. Ten years later the Low Mill followed. Population in Skipton was 2305 in 1801, 3411 in 1821 but by 1831 had jumped to 4802, an increase connected with the completion of the Leeds and Liverpool Canal across the summit length in 1816, and the opening of more factories, some of them for cotton. The population was nearly stable through the next twenty years and then began its great increase in response to the invasion of the cotton industry and the building of nearly all the larger mills between 1850 and 1880. The increase, speeding up after 1851, became greatest between 1871 and 1911, more than doubling the population, from 6078 to 12,974.

Every available space in the old town had been built upon and between 1860 and 1890, a completely new Middletown Ward was built to the south-east joining to, and associated with, the mills which were built along the canal banks. This is an area of close-set terraces of small houses—parlour, kitchen-scullery and two bedrooms; back yard but no gardens. This area expanded between 1890 and 1910 by peripheral addition so that there is now, the large area of Middletown and New Town, the later houses still in parallel rows, but slightly larger and with a small strip of front garden to many of them. At the same time as these developments, the town's Mill Fields west of the head of High Street were built up, but with a little more diversity created by the presénce of the Wesleyan Day Schools and Chapel, and the Catholic school and chapel. Part of the fields was taken by the new Ermystead's Grammar School and grounds, opened in 1877 when the old grammar school became too small, and by St Monica's Convent. These buildings with their large grounds made a pleasant boundary to the closely built-up area. [2]

By 1911 the town had become stabilised and its population of almost 13,000 (12,974) dropped a little and was not recovered until 1951 when it reached 13,207, then dropping to 13,008 in 1961. This, however, does not mean that the town has stagnated. Large areas of the older, inadequate property have been cleared and big estates of new housing have been built on the east and south-east sides, while at the same time there has been removal into surrounding villages which lie in the Rural District. The commercial activity of the town has increased but the additional employment has been balanced by the increased habit of living in the rural area, made possible by the advent of the motor car and public transport. Nearby villages such as Embsay, Carleton, Gargrave, and others have an increasing number of residents who work in Skipton.

The latest change in the town is its growing importance as a tourist centre—"the Gateway to the Dales" (National Park) and the most convenient place for a meal or shopping stop on the way to and from the Lakes, or to and from the coasts. The industries, though active, are hidden along the canal zone, the market for sheep and cattle is increasing in importance but is on the fringe of the town near the railway station. The town centre is now almost entirely de-

[2] A. and S. E. Raistrick, *Skipton: a study in site value,* 1930.

Yorkshire Post

Plate 25 Halifax. Worsted and carpet mills fill up the bottom of the Hebble valley. Industrial housing on the gentler parts of the hillside. The numerous mill chimneys are an interesting monument to the steam age.

Plate 26 Kellingley Colliery, the latest and most modernised pit. Knottingley to Goole main road and the railway flank it. The Aire and Calder Canal is seen in top right (faintly). Looking towards

Plate 27 Sheffield City Hall, 1932, part of the new city centre plan. Typical of good building in Yorkshire stone.

Plate 28 New housing near the centre of Sheffield, replacing industrial slums. Top left, an area of 'between the wars' semi-detached housing.

voted to commerce and the tourist trade, and keeps much of its character as a small country market town. The plan of the High Street and central part is still essentially that of the sixteenth century, for although the buildings have been replaced more than once, their successors have remained over the same foundations (Fig. 12).

Ripon is the other true market town, smaller than Skipton, with a population of 10,486 in 1961, and in some ways comparable. The mediaeval town had two foci, the Minster and the market place (Plate 23). Kirkgate connected these and other streets; Allhallows Gate, St Mary Gate, and Fishergate make the framework of the old town centre with a short extension of housing along the main roads leaving this square, Stone Bridge Gate (bridge over the river Ure) West Gate, Blossom Gate, St Anns Gate, Skelgate, Bondgate, and the Horse Fair. The town is built on the north bank of the river Skell and some half mile south of the river Ure.[3] Although the town had some fame for its woollen manufactures in the fourteenth and fifteenth centuries, these had declined in the sixteenth century. The fairs for horses, horned cattle, and sheep became the principal centre of the town trade, along with the regular markets which served a very large rural area. Tanning and leather working linked naturally with the fairs. The early plan of the town is still clear; little change has been made beyond a filling-in by building on the gardens and by the addition of a broad fringe of Victorian and Edwardian 'villa' building. The most important recent expansion is a large area south of the river Skell, and an 'estate' at Clotherholme on the north-west edge of the town.

In both Ripon and Skipton the stages of growth of the town are easily detected if a study of the maps is combined with close inspection of the actual buildings, and many

[3] There is an excellent plan of Ripon in J. Jefferies, *The County of Yorkshire surveyed*, 1771, Plate I (see Fig. 13).

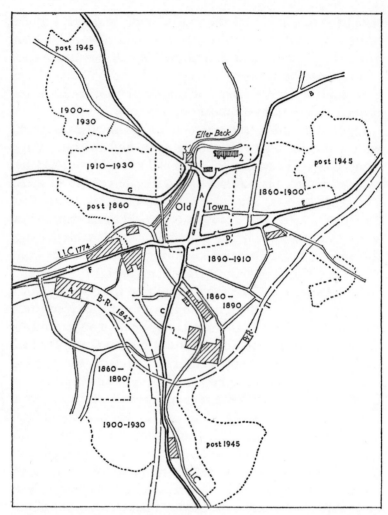

Fig. 12. Skipton. Dates indicate approximate period of building up these areas. Cross hatched buildings are the various mills and the railway station.

A. High Street. B. Harrogate road. C. Keighley road. D. Newmarket Street. E. Otley road. F. Broughton road. G. Gargrave road. 1. Church. 2. Castle. 3. Corn Mill. 4. Railway Station.

parallels with the other rural market towns will be recognised. They are both linked with a wide service area by the roads and the motor bus transport system operating from the town as a centre.

In the congested textile area many of the places which were only large villages with a domestic woollen industry in the early eighteenth century grew at such a rate in the nineteenth as to become cities, county, and municipal boroughs with populations approaching or exceeding 100,000. Bradford, with a population in 1961 of 295,922, Dewsbury 52,963, Halifax 96,120, Huddersfield 130,652, Leeds 510,676, and Wakefield 61,268, are County Boroughs, each the centre of a large number of wards, most of them former villages on th periphery of the old town. They form a lattice over the textile area, with a number of Municipal Boroughs, Batley, Brighouse, Morley, Ossett, Pudsey, and Spenborough, of 30,000 to 40,000 population, spread among them. Still filling in the conurbation there are a few Urban Districts, Elland, Hebden Royd, Heckmondwyke, Mirfield, and Sowerby Bridge, none of them reaching 20,000 population; and finally there is, as a background, the small Rural District of Hepton in the head of the Calder valley, with its four villages and parishes of Blackshaw, Erringden, Heptonstall, and Wadsworth and a total population of only 4088. Even with this vast concentration of towns, the topography of the area—the deep cut valleys of Aire, Calder, and Colne across which the textile area sprawls are separated by high and often wild moors, with many deep cut, well wooded tributary valleys often almost ravines, all these features relieve the network of towns and leave very few of them beyond easy reach of lovely or wild country (Plate 24).

The amazing growth of these towns and cities follows the mechanisation of the many textile processes, the advent of steam power and the rapid development of communications,

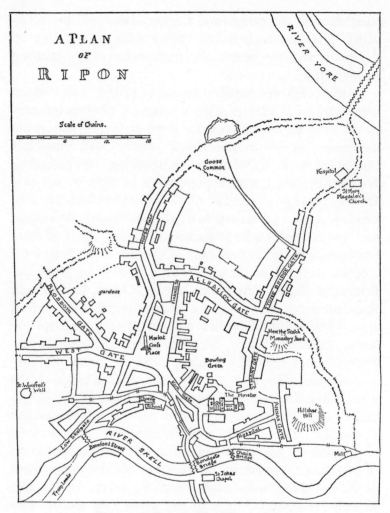

Fig. 13. Jefferies' plan of Ripon, 1771.

164

first canals, then railways and later, motor transport by a network of better roads. Some of the cities have an old town centre with a long history, Halifax and Wakefield in particular having a claim to early importance.

Halifax, the centre of an enormous parish, had become the centre of a woollen industry of purely domestic type by the fifteenth century. As early as 1414 the Court Rolls refer to a Tenter Croft and in the same century there were two fulling mills mentioned at Rastrick. By the mid-sixteenth century Halifax was the centre of a sufficient wool and cloth trade to merit the so-called Halifax Acts relieving the clothiers of the restrictions on their trade imposed by the legislation on behalf of the wool Staple.[4] The Act of 1555 mentions in its preamble "above 500 households there [Halifax] newly increased within these forty years past". It established the 'wool drivers' and 'broggers' who brought wool from a wide countryside into the Halifax market, as described already (Chapter 5). This increase in the early part of the sixteenth century was maintained throughout the large parish which included at that time most of upper Calderdale, so that by 1580 the population of the parish was estimated at 12,000. By 1763 it was 41,220 and in 1871, 173,313, of whom more than 65,000 were in the town of Halifax. Looking to the town itself, its early growth was almost entirely due to the importance of its corn, wool, and cloth markets. The town lies on the western slope of the Hebble valley, the east side being too steep for building, being even yet almost free of any usage. The large stream was soon utilised for power and the four miles of it from Lee Bridge on the northern edge of the old town, down to the junction with the Calder, supplied power to twenty-four mills. Eleven were corn mills, an evidence of its importance as a corn market for a wide area. There were

[4]Passed following complaints against an Act of 1532 which limited wool dealing to members of the Staple only.

eight fulling mills connected with the cloth trade, four others serving dyeing and finishing processes, and one iron forge.[5]

With the advent of steam power it was this valley which became the location of large worsted mills, with the building of which went the first and major expansion of the town (Plate 25). Until the mid-nineteenth century, housing needs had been met by town infilling, but, with the great increase in labour demanded by the mills, shown in the Census figures—1861, 37,014 and 1871, 65,124 (the latter figure including a small boundary increase, insignificant, however, in the total figure), an era of industrial housing began on the west of the town. This extension was largely of close-set rows of small industrial housing, and stands out clearly on the town map.

A notable feature of all the textile towns is the large amount of fine building in stone which accompanied the expansion of the second half of the nineteenth century. The emerging municipalities built impressive town halls, designed by famous architects and embodying the highest skill of the stone mason exerted on some of the world's finest building stone from the local quarries which were part of a great industry. Whatever modern taste may say of Victorian Gothic and pseudo-classic, the town halls and other buildings, Trade Halls, Wool Exchanges, and the larger chapels, warehouses, and mills, exhibit both splendid design and craftsmanship, along with a high degree of municipal pride which made this zone a treasury of functional architecture. Much of this work is being cleared for glass and concrete erections which have little individuality and none of the sense of stability and pride of the older stone structures. However, sufficient of the old still remains and a feeling for preservation of such buildings as Leeds and Bradford Town Halls, and Huddersfield Railway Station

[5] T. W. Hanson, *The Story of Halifax*, 1920.

among many other buildings, is growing. The new town centres, to the older generations, seem to be undistinguished mazes of almost identical multi-storey blocks, supermarkets, giant road roundabouts, and subways, with nothing to distinguish Sheffield from Halifax or Bradford unless one can catch a glimpse through some concrete canyon of a fragment of the friendly hills which used to seem so near and refreshing. The relief of discovering the outline and some remains of the old town centre and reminders of its life and history is an ample reward for all the time and study taken for the search and this cannot be recommended too strongly.

The position of Halifax as chief town of the worsted industry declined and was taken over by Bradford in the last decades of the nineteenth century. After a period of stability when Halifax had comparatively little new building, it began in the 1920's in particular to expand with much new building on the ridge to the north of the town, between the Hebble Brook and the Strines Beck, and in smaller estates on the western fringe. All the larger towns show these fringe estates of greater or less extent dating between the wars and post war, and indistinguishable one from another. There is as much uniformity in this building as there is in the most typical of the nineteenth century industrial housing.

Barnsley during the last century has been synonymous with coal, a town pre-eminently associated with the coal trade, collieries, and colliers. This was not always so, and today changes are taking place which have shifted the centres of coal production to the east of the town. A writer in 1918 said, "It needs little observation, anywhere about Barnsley, to see that the town itself and its whole neighbourhood are entirely devoted to coal-mining. Every village in the outskirts is a colliery village; the streets, roads and lanes are for ever thronged with miners, going to and

167

from the various pits . . . the most important building in Barnsley itself is the fine block which houses the officials and staff of the Miners' Association." This, however, would no longer be entirely true, nor was it true for any but the nineteenth century. In the fourteenth century Barnsley was a woollen town, standing high in the Ulnagers' rolls and paying tax on woollen cloths at a rate comparable with Doncaster, Selby, and Skipton. In 1475 these places had disappeared from the ulnage accounts but Barnsley had increased from the twenty-six pieces taxed in 1396 to 142 pieces. Barnsley and neighbouring hamlets remained as an area of handloom weaving for several centuries. In the eighteenth century these trades changed from woollen to linen weaving, and with this developed flax spinning and bleaching. In the first quarter of the nineteenth century the linen manufacture was an important part of the town's economy; a directory of 1822 lists thirty-two linen manu-facturers, a flax spinner and nine linen and woollen drapers. Another trade of long standing was wire drawing, the steel wire being produced largely for needle-making.

The town had markets and fairs which for several centuries had been important assets for a wide rural area, and which in the eighteenth and nineteenth centuries catered not only to the rural needs but to a growing popu-lation of iron and coal workers. The South Yorkshire charcoal-iron industry which flourished in the late seven-teenth and early eighteenth centuries supplied the raw material for the wire drawing trade which served two dominant groups of customers, the comb makers for the wool combing and carding, and the needle makers. For a time Barnsley held a leading position in this latter section of the trade. Both the textile and the iron trades were domestic industries until the nineteenth century, and were carried on in small workshops attached to the cottages, where at most, only one or two people could work.

The general aspect of the town remained that of any other small market town until an expansion and change in the coal industry in the second half of the eighteenth century began a period of expansion. This change was due to a widening demand for coal. Until 1750 the coal was won only for the local demand, mainly domestic and in very small quantity for the wire smithies. By 1800 coal was in demand over a wide area and markets were being discovered as far away as York and Hull.

The improvement in mining techniques enabled the miners to follow the valuable and thick Barnsley seam to greater depths. By 1800 Barnsley was the centre town of a rich coalfield and plans were being made for the construction of canals to carry the coal to the Humber and to all parts of the North. In the 1830's there was a marked development of pits to the east as deeper shafts became possible. The steady eastward dip was taking the Silkstone and Barnsley coals to greater depths and by 1890 collieries had been started right up to the Magnesian Limestone belt, and the concealed coalfield, beneath a surface cover of rocks later than the Coal Measures, was ready for exploitation. This development of the coalfield was accompanied by a rapid expansion of the town from 1830 onwards, and the increasing population was accommodated in housing areas which soon enclosed the old town centre. By 1869 the population had increased to about 23,000 and Barnsley was raised to the status of a County Borough. The population was over 50,000 by 1911 and 75,000 by 1951. The increased housing, however, was very compact and Barnsley remains a compact town with very little sprawl of recent housing estates in its fringes.

The greater part of Barnsley's post-war housing needs has been met in large estates on its periphery. Gawber village a mile to the north-west has now a large modern housing estate; Worsborough Common on the southern edge, what is almost a new town between Barnsley and Stairfoot, the developments at Lundwood and Athersley, all these form a ring of large housing estates dependent upon Barnsley for their cultural and commercial life.

The twentieth century saw the sinking of much deeper pits on the concealed coalfield under the lowland agricultural area east of the Magnesian Limestone. These collieries were very deep and to match the heavy capital cost, needed larger areas of coal to work. There emerged a new landscape of a rich rural countryside with widespaced and isolated new collieries of a very large size (Plate 26). Inevitably the labour for the pits was before long housed in new villages and towns built at the pit head, not enclosing, but often adjacent to, an old village centre. The population figures illustrate this creation of new towns in striking fashion. Maltby in 1911 had a population of 1700, but in 1921 this had jumped to 7531. Near Doncaster, Edlington with 580 in 1911, had 5298 in 1921. The Maltby shaft was sunk in 1910; Askern in 1912 took its population from just under 1000 to 2729 in 1921. The most easterly pit, Thorne, was only sunk in 1926 but shows the same jump in population, 6076 in 1921, and 14,462 in 1951. This pit was closed in the 1950's but population increased slowly to 15,280 in 1961, partly by the increase of local industries but largely because of transport into Doncaster which enabled it to become a dormitory town for people with work there.

There is a progression to be seen in these new colliery towns. The earlier ones have high density areas of terrace houses, not very different from the later development in the textile towns; but in the inter-war years and the post-war period, expansion of the new colliery centres followed the more popular lines of curving 'avenues' and 'drives', with houses at a much lower density. The small groups of two or four houses with gardens and often with road verges set with grass and trees, follow the common suburban pattern of their time. The number of these new towns associated with collieries in the country between Barnsley and Doncaster is at least a dozen, while south of Doncaster there are at least another half-dozen. Those nearest to Doncaster have been partly increased as overspill areas and this, with the colliery increase, accounts for such a rise as Bentley: 1911, 6497; 1921, 12,941; by 1951 19,837 and 1961, 22,961. Only a close analysis would separate this steady increase between mining, the other occupations, and dormitory residence.

Doncaster, which has a very long history as an important market town, claiming a Roman origin as the bridge or ford across the Don at the camp of Danum, suffered an almost complete rebuilding in the very prosperous years of the later nineteenth century. However, the centre around the markets and parish church retains the mediaeval street plan and names. The town was described by Defoe in 1727 as a "noble and spacious town, exceeding populous". Some of its importance came from its position on the Great North Road, a junction from which served many of the south Yorkshire towns. It became an important railway junction and was chosen in 1853 as the site of the engineering workshops of the Great Northern Railway. Though many other industries have been added, and in this century there has been a shift of the emphasis on coal from Barnsley towards Doncaster, to most people it still stands out as a great railway town. By 1871 its population was nearly 19,000 and it was the commercial and market centre of a wide and rich rural area. The development of collieries in the twentieth century brought a large population within its sphere, and more and more this population has come to regard and to use Doncaster as its shopping and service centre, for goods, entertainment, and professional services of all kinds.

The old centre of the town, now largely Victorian,

171

stands back from and above the river banks. These accommodate a broad industrial belt which stretches for four miles along the south bank and is in fact only a part of the industrialised Don valley which extends from Sheffield right to Thorne Marsh. The industrial housing of the late nineteenth century filled in all spaces in the town and extended in solid masses across the low ground between river and town, in the high density areas of Wheatley Park and Hexthorpe. The larger Victorian and Edwardian housing was mainly on slightly higher ground and an area between Bessecar and Cantley, south-east of the old town and only two miles from the centre, was developed. Inter-war and post-war housing has gone largely to the small hamlets on the outskirts such as Armthorpe and Edenthorpe.

Doncaster town is within the clay belt of the lower Don valley and near the great flats of the Vale of Trent. It lacks any good building stone within easy reach, so it, and its surrounding estates, are all brick-built. The brick belt extends north-east to Thorne and beyond, and in the older rural housing is marked by a wide use of red pantile roofing materials.

Some early stages in the growth of Sheffield have been discussed in Chapter 2 (pp. 55–6) but we need to look now at the growth of the present city and at some of its features. For many centuries the town has been famous for its manufactures of cutlery and edged tools, and by the beginning of the eighteenth century it had got an almost complete monopoly of this trade. The old town centre and the steep valleys nearby were crowded with the small workshops and homes of cutlers, and many water-wheels were harnessed to the wheels of grinders and finishers. By 1750 the population was estimated to be about 15,000 so that it was by then to be reckoned as a considerable town. In and about 1740 two inventions started a rapid expansion in Sheffield trades. Thomas Boulsover discovered a practical method of producing a silver-plated copper sheet from which was made the beautiful Old Sheffield Plate, now so rare and highly valued. At the same time Benjamin Huntsman was discovering how to make crucible (cast) steel, and gave impetus to what was to become Sheffield's largest modern industry, the production of special steels. When Bessemer's process for making steel in bulk became available in 1863 the steel industry was able to expand at a phenomenal rate. The town had grown large enough to be incorporated as a Borough in 1843, and by 1888, with a population around 300,000, it became a County Borough, then a City in 1893. By 1911 it was the largest city in Yorkshire with 460,185 inhabitants. This growth has continued until in 1951 the population exceeded half a million. By area it is today the fourth largest city in Britain. The comparative stability of the population figures since 1921 and the small decline between 1951 and 1961 is due not to any stagnation in the city but to the coming of the private motor car. This new transport has tempted more and more of the folk who work in Sheffield to make their homes just outside the city boundaries in Derbyshire, still within easy reach of all the city amenities.

The great prosperity of the city in the last quarter of the nineteenth century and its new dignity as County Borough and City led to the creation of civic buildings which are among the finest in Yorkshire. As these are grouped close together they form a natural civic centre, which, as the clearance of inferior buildings and the realisation of the city's development plan continues, will make this one of the finest cities in the country.

An outstanding older building is the Cutlers' Hall, built in 1832 with later extensions. As befits the importance of the cutlers in the city's history and present position, the Hall is of very dignified design and elegant interior. The Town Hall (1890–7) has a fine tower and with the extensions of 1923 makes an excellent focus around which the new Civic Centre will be grouped. The Law Courts, Arts Centre, and Civic Theatre, are associated with it and close at hand are the City Hall (1932) and the Central Library and Graves Art Gallery (1934) (Plate 27). The new markets on the Castle site and other building in progress are in scale and design entirely suited to the new city centre now rising on the area formerly occupied by tiny houses and workshops which had declined to a slum condition.

As the cutlers and others prospered they built their new houses in large park-like gardens on the hill ridges rising from the city centre, leaving the valleys largely unaltered. Sheffield thus got a large suburban area, well wooded, with low density, high quality houses and many mansions. In recent years the mansions have been adapted to hotels, guest houses and other such purposes, and the spacious grounds of some of them have provided sites for schools, university hostels and many other buildings of public character. In the last few decades the Corporation have planned and built several estates of houses, and de-signed several schools and other buildings which have attracted attention and commendation throughout the world of planners (Plate 28). Some of this work foreshadows the shape of the future towns and can be left for mention in the next chapter. A splendid feature of Sheffield is its Green Belt, which, because of the topography, with high ridges and steep sided, narrow valleys, offers a ten-mile circuit of woodland and country paths, wooded valleys, and splendid ridges offering spectacular views over the city.

The city has a few old buildings of historic interest, but its chief appeal is the urgent sense of change and transfor-mation, the realisation of a plan which is taking every advantage of the site and of the advantages given by a period of great prosperity and civic pride during the latter part of last century and the early decades of this.

BIBLIOGRAPHY

Burn, D. *Economic History of Steelmaking 1867–1939*, Cambridge, 1940.
Burn, D. *The Steel Industry, 1939–59*, Cambridge, 1961.
Neff, J. U. *The Rise of the British Coal Industry*, 2 vols., London, 1932.
Beresford, M. W. and Jones, G. R. (Eds.). *Leeds and its Region*, British Association Report, Leeds, 1967.
British Association Report, *Sheffield and its Region*, Sheffield, 1956.

8. A new landscape: late twentieth century

The planned future: Housing and new towns. Motorways, airfields, etc. Power landscape: pylons, power stations. New agriculture.
Countryside Bill, National Parks, Rural Development Board, Humber–Yorks Development Board.

IN A PREVIOUS chapter some reference has been made to the revolution in building in the sixteenth and seventeenth centuries by which the timber houses and buildings which had been the common mediaeval type were replaced by buildings of a new construction in stone. Villages and farms, though still on the same foundations, took on a new aspect through new methods of construction and new fashions in architecture, and these spread slowly through the whole country. In the Industrial Revolution one of the accompanying features of the technical innovations was the vast spread of industrial housing, especially in the nineteenth century, which converted many villages into towns and towns into cities. In some of the towns the main change in building materials was seen in the increased use of brick and Welsh slate for cheapness where stone and stone slates had been the earlier tradition.[1] Construction was essentially the same although planning was meaner and the density of housing was greatly increased.

In this twentieth century we have been thrust into the

---

[1] The extra cost of stone was largely in the wages of the skilled masons needed to cut and dress it.

Plate 29 New style blocks of flats in Leeds, steel, glass and concrete.

Plate 30 The new M1 road, cutting through the Don valley industrial belt, on the Tinsley viaduct.

Plate 31   Ferrybridge power station on the river Calder.

G. D. Bolton

Central Electricity Generating Board

Plate 32 400 keV electricity distributing line from the Thorpe Marsh power station (seen in the right distance). This is the line from Thorpe Marsh to Stalybridge.

opening scenes of a far more radical revolution which involves every aspect of building, materials, design, and lay-out along with larger problems of planning on both local and regional scales. The crowded areas of small dwellings which are inadequate to meet the newer health standards, are being cleared away in all our towns and cities, and their place is being taken in part by high density blocks of multistorey flats towering above lawns and open spaces (Plates 28 and 29). Shopping and commercial premises follow a similar pattern, and stone and brick is being replaced in most towns by concrete and glass. The centres of our cities, Leeds, Bradford, Sheffield, and others, are being redesigned—old streets and buildings have been ruthlessly demolished and a centre of new streets and traffic ways, with multistorey buildings has taken their places among which an occasional handsome and now alien building of Victorian splendour may survive and afford a landmark to a lost and puzzled older generation. We are witnessing a rapid change in the city 'landscape' in which the prime change is one of scale, and increasing verticality.

The new office blocks offer a terrible monotony of small repeated units set on a vertical plane, as unimaginative and dreary as the streets of small identical houses we are getting rid of. More light and easier cleaning are the chief attractions but whether it be offices or flats, scores or hundreds of identical units repeat the regularity of a honeycomb and thousands of folk must now mould their living and working hours within identical small boxes, looking to their leisure hours for the experience of a diversified environment. A greater efficiency in the use of living and working space is increasing with every new building, but individual character and privacy are retreating. The ingenuity of many an architect seems to be challenged by the child's game of piling identical rectangular 'building bricks' units into diverse patterns which have rejected all curves and which cannot

M

get away from the unattractive form of a cigar box set on end.

Among public buildings there is more diversity— libraries, theatres, lecture halls, offer shapes in far greater variety. In the public buildings more and more blank walls, adorned by symbolic sculptures which need an explanatory leaflet for their comprehension, enclose a world of perpetual artificial lighting and 'conditioned' air. None the less, all the portents are towards more interesting cities suited to a new age, designed to allow a freer movement and better accommodation for larger populations. Already cities are acquiring a skyline which at first is a little startling. Where one used to catch an occasional glimpse in the distance of a rounded hill shoulder, we now see an assembly of 'tower' flats, sometimes most effectively grouped though apt to bring to mind some of the finest of the Victorian landscaped 'follies'. Skylines within the city have achieved a greater and more attractive diversity, and upward growth has allowed the creation of new areas of lawn and open space. The older generation is bound to grumble and to feel lost in a strangely foreign world, but the new generations are being offered a finer environment in which to live and work.

The problem which threatens to get out of hand and which is a powerful influence in the redesign of the cities, is that of the explosive increase in the number of motor cars and lorries. The exclusion of this traffic from sections of the new cities, or its very rigid control, is allowing an entirely new freedom in the design and landscaping of pedestrian precincts, shopping centres and so forth. Area developments such as the university campus or other groupings of buildings with a special functional connection are creating park-like areas of open space which are giving the new cities a diversity of landscape which no old city has possessed. None the less the present trends, so far as they can be judged, are towards the emphasis of the town and city boundary. The early twentieth century sprawl of suburbia with its ribbon developments forming a twilight zone by which town faded into a region of neither town nor country only to coagulate into the next town is now being more rigidly controlled. This sprawl has in many areas developed beyond present redemption, but it will not be continued or repeated. Town and country are regaining their character as different and distinct environments, complementary to one another.

An outstanding new element in the late twentieth century scene will be provided by the road and motorway system now in the early stages of construction. The canal and rail systems of the eighteenth and nineteenth centuries followed the valleys and helped to concentrate factories and growing towns along the valley bottoms. The new transport lines have been drawn with much more regard to a regional development plan than to the local topography. While the canals and railways hunted for passes by which to get through the high barrier of the Pennines, one new motorway is planned and is being built as the TransPennine Way. Its line is directly across the high moors and summits—modern constructional methods can smooth out all merely local hills and valleys—cuttings and embankments can create long and easy gradients over miles of country seamed with steep-sided mountain streams, and the new earthmoving machines can indeed approach very near to moving mountains.

The older road systems grew largely out of local needs and the longer roads across the breadth of the county were made in most cases by improving the linked-up lengths of older roads. The roads 'grew' by customary usage and the turnpikes regularised them. Now we have a system of new roads which is being planned nationally to supply rapid transport lines across the length and breadth of the country (Plate 30). In many ways it is a repetition of the pattern of the main line express routes of the railways with the difference that hilly country does not prohibit the new type of road, and that the advance in mechanical handling and removal of rock materials has outstripped the wildest dreams of the nineteenth century civil engineers whose most powerful tool was the muscular strength of the navvy. The new road pattern of the West Riding must be integrated into the national road pattern in such a way that local traffic can flow smoothly and rapidly and can also make an efficient contact with and entry on to the national traffic lines.

The basic plan which the authorities see as developing and maturing in the West Riding during the next quarter century will hinge on the north to south national motorway M1, and an improved A1 with a new east to west Trans-Pennine motorway from these roads, across the textile area and the high Pennines to Manchester. Extensions of this road, M62, will go to Goole and Hull in Yorkshire and to Liverpool in Lancashire. It will also make connections with the north to south motorways on each side of the Pennines. A second TransPennine motorway is planned a little to the south to link the coal-steel areas with south Lancashire. The motorways are, for the greater part, new creations, entirely new features imposed on an old landscape. Their own particuar landscape will be created in a way which no older road ever demanded. The junctions where they connect with one another and cross will rank in size and complexity with some of the largest engineered structures in the country. They will cover more land than a large village.

Though the new roads will serve the centres of industry and population, there can be no roadside development. Industrial estates, towns and villages must be related to connecting roads, and the motorway will stand naked and exposed through all its length, striding across the country, a new feature in its own right. Perhaps the Romano-British native, when he saw the major Roman roads stretching through his countryside, ignoring merely local interests, part of an Imperial strategy he never understood, experienced something which no other generations until our own can share. We, on our approach as pedestrians to a new motor-way, are little changed from his position; allowing for greater sophistication we have jumped the centuries and look on a revolution which in basic essentials has much in common with that on which he looked, an alien line of transport.

The technical revolution of the post-war years with its amazing increase in industrial output has created a vastly greater demand for power, supplied to a new pattern. At the opening of this century coal was still brought to the in-dividual mills and factories, burned there, and its energy used for raising steam. Steam engines which were the pride of their owners as well as of their 'tenters', were individual, christened with names, cared for and admired for their silent power and efficiency. The engine house was the heart of the factory, an architectural focal point in the building with its associated symbol, the mill chimney. This has all changed —a mill engine is now a rarity—electricity has displaced it. Power is now itemised through an army of electric motors and the engine house has given way to the distribution switchboard. The electric energy is generated in bulk at a few enormous power stations and distributed by a grid of overhead power lines which embrace the whole country (Plate 31).

These high-tension power lines are a feature of the new landscape which we have to accept and get used to accept-ing. There are a few places where the demands of amenity are very high where these lines may be undergrounded for a relatively short distance, but the overwhelming majority will remain above ground. Pylons stride across the country-side with their lace-like structure, each of them a smaller, daintier Eiffel Tower, with the fine connecting catenaries of wire, showing as silver lines where the sun catches them. The long succession of pylons and their wires is not without a delicate beauty of its own, but in some landscapes it can become an alien line—a ruled and sternly regulated line drawn across a countryside of rolling hill shapes, winding streams, natural curves. There will be places in our new landscape where power lines can become acceptable but there are some where they will be obtrusive and where thought, skill, and appreciation of natural beauty will have to be devoted to the selection of a tolerable line (Plate 32).

The power stations at the multiple hearts of the grid are introducing a new dimension and new shapes into the scene. Whether energised by coal, oil, or atomic fuels, the prime demand is for cooling water. This binds the power station to the larger riversides or estuaries in the lowland part of their course. The cluster of gigantic concrete cooling towers with their graceful parabolic profile and the slender plume of vapour at their summit is now the architectural symbol of power. In most cases set down in an agricultural area, they can only stand as monumental structures not to be hidden or to suffer camouflage, but to become acceptable by their functional beauty and architectural merit.

The derelict remains of earlier industries, colliery waste heaps, the crumbled remains of coke ovens, the slag heaps and scorched areas of ironworks and the debased areas of ponds and flooded subsidences occupy many areas of the Riding. Government help and encouragement is now available and the planners are at work redeeming this land as quickly as means and labour will allow. What fresh landscape will the next generation find where we found desolation? Pit heaps can be levelled and subsidences filled in. Land for housing or industry will emerge from some waste areas. Other areas can be returned to agriculture and some will be landscaped into recreational areas. Sports fields, ponds for boating, even quiet areas for the enjoyment of natural life, will emerge, and all this will not be a restoration of a former landscape but the creation of a new one, fashioned in the idiom of the twentieth and twenty-first centuries.

The population of this country has increased so that now there is only three-quarters of an acre per person if equally shared. With this scarcity of land, and with recreation becoming more and more an essential in modern life, it appears that cities and towns will have to accept a higher density of occupation in order to relieve rural areas from the blight of a thinly spread surburbia. The compaction is already starting with the high density flats, and the creation of a more definite edge to towns will also help. Recreation will have to be provided by a large measure of the multiple usage of land where some forms of agriculture, particularly rough grazing can be combined with access for outdoor recreations like walking, where forestry can be combined with recreational use, and where the large areas of reservoir catchments and the reservoirs themselves can be made available for public enjoyment. All this and more has been recognised, and will be implemented through the provisions of the Countryside Bill of 1968.

Alongside the new town landscapes the Bill provides the means of creating Country Parks, not far from the towns, areas easy of access, and reserved for public recreation. These will be areas of wild or semi-wild land, or parklands of earlier creation, with woods, water, grassy areas, and the minimum of service buildings, into which areas people can drive their cars, can picnic, walk, boat, play games, and enjoy themselves in a good country environment. Part of the Studley Royal and Fountains Abbey estate will make such a park—others are being planned and in due course will be designated. These lungs will provide something of what the average townsman is looking for when he leaves the town in his car and takes a long journey in search of country where he can relax and enjoy himself. The aim will be to find the traveller what he wants without imposing on him a long car journey by overcrowded roads to some area where he is unable to find room for picnics, games, or other enjoyments except in a few crowded spots.

Country Parks will soon occupy the place in the landscape which the private parks occupied in the eighteenth and nineteenth centuries, and will most likely preserve some of the best of them in the process. In their creation and management there is the opportunity for experiments in landscaping and land usage, in preservation or even creation of amenity on a scale only realised before by a few of the greatest of the landscape gardeners. The driving purpose, however, offers a great contrast. Against the ensuring of privacy for a wealthy family and its guests we must now place the making of an area in which large numbers, hundreds, or even thousands of everyday, working people can be absorbed; a place where they can find varied recreations amidst natural beauty, without the overcrowding and noise that would more properly belong to a fairground. What a splendid problem for the planners' skill and ingenuity and what an asset to our town populations this idea offers.

Among other aspects of the new landscape two stabilising features remain to be mentioned—National Parks and Forestry. After many years of thought and pressure the National Parks and Access to the Countryside Act of 1949 enabled the creation of ten National Parks, one of which, the Yorkshire Dales Park, has more than half its area of 690 square miles in the West Riding, while part of the south-west of the Riding comes within the boundary of the Peak Park. After designation the Act charges the Park Planning Committee with the duty of "the preservation and enhancement of natural beauty . . . and for encouraging the provision or improvement, for persons resorting to National Parks, of facilities for the enjoyment thereof and for the enjoyment of the opportunities for open air recreation and the study of nature afforded thereby." There is a possibility of mutual embarrassment between these two aims. The increase of motor traffic and facility for people to get into the National Park is already creating demands for facilities which could seriously threaten or altogether prevent the preservation of the natural beauty and disturb some of the wild life which naturalists wish to study.

The landscape as we know it is the result of centuries of human activity and of slow adaptations. Roads, walls, hedges, fields, and plantations, many of the grasses and vegetation are the product of human endeavour. The land has never been static, but a progressive change has gone on steadily, almost imperceptibly and has been accepted by each generation as a legacy from the previous one. Change must and will still go on, but today the rate of change has accelerated beyond all expectation and threatens to overwhelm us in its speed and magnitude. It will take wise planning and controls to prevent short term expediency taking over and doing and allowing things which would in the end destroy the countryside. Decisions will be based upon knowledge much of which has still to be gained by detailed studies and surveys. If right decisions are taken we can expect an efficient control of the developing landscape which could make it as acceptable to future generations for its beauty and harmony, as the present countryside is to us.

The increasing necessity for greater timber resources is being met by the Forestry Commission which in the course of its work is transforming many landscapes. To the present time, they have had little effect in the West Riding, but in the next few decades it is fairly certain that some of our higher ground, and more acceptably, some of the upland stream courses and cloughs, will carry new woodlands. Some landscapes will be enhanced by judicious plantations and possibly a small forest will be established on what is now high moorland. The new Rural Development Board has power to amalgamate small and uneconomic hill farms, to improve rough upland, and to assist agriculture by the association with it of forestry occupations. The pace of all these changes is so great that any prediction of the future beyond the next few years and in the most general terms, would be foolhardy. The most one can say is that never has there been so much legislation providing for the preservation and enhancement of our environment as there is now and never so much need to avoid over-hasty and expedient solutions for our problems. The most certain fact of all is that just as the scene has changed progressively through the past centuries, so it will continue to change in the future. Study, planning, and controls may make the future changes more acceptable than some which took place in the recent past.

BIBLIOGRAPHY

West Riding County Council, 'A growth policy for the North', *County Development Plan*, second revision, 1966.
Abrahams, H. M. *Britain's National Parks*, London, 1959. (*The Yorkshire Dales*, Raistrick, A.)

Index

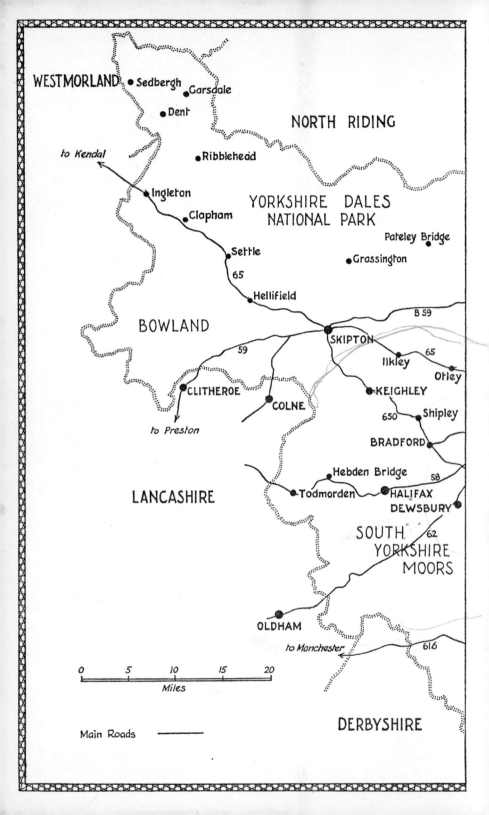